WINSTON
The Life of a Gun Dog

WINSTON

The Life of a Gun Dog

Ben O. Williams

WILLOW CREEK PRESS

© 2003 Ben O. Williams

Published by Willow Creek Press
P.O. Box 147, Minocqua, Wisconsin 54548
www.willowcreekpress.com

Library of Congress Cataloging-in-Publication Data

Williams, Ben O.
    Winston : the life of a bird dog / By Ben O. Williams.
        p. cm.
    ISBN 1-57223-705-8 (alk. paper)
    1. Brittany spaniel--Biography. 2. Bird dogs--Biography. 3.
Williams, Ben O. I. Title
    SF429.B78W55 2003
    636.752--dc22

                                                        2003016315

Printed in Canada

Dedication
*This book owes thanks to all the dogs I've
shared my life with over the years.*

Acknowledgments
*These stories are all true, but instead of using
the real names of the people involved and
recognizable landmarks, I've chosen to substitute
fictitious names and places to protect our favorite
cherished bird covers. I owe a special thanks
to a host of friends who were participants
in these stories. You know who you are,
and the places we hunted together.*

Contents

Preface

The name Ben O. Williams paints a picture for all of us who have hunted birds behind pointing dogs in the grasslands of the West. The picture that Ben's name evokes is that of a dignified man in well-worn hunting clothes, walking unhurriedly in ankle-high grass towards an abandoned homestead. There, half a dozen American Brittany's, spread over an acre of land, focus on the lead dog. Over the centuries, the prairie winds have smoothed out the rough places, leaving an undulating and inviting landscape of short grass and sagebrush. On this late fall day, shadows appear painted to one side of the weather-beaten buildings; smaller shadows spring from under the feet of the dogs. All classic examples of their kind, the Brittany's stand at attention, oblivious to everything save their objective. A redtailed hawk sails in an immense blue sky on a thermal hundreds of feet above; a good place to regard infinity.

Hunting without a dog is, to Ben's mind, an empty exercise. He has trained Brittanys for fifty years and his dogs are as famous in the West as Elhew pointers are legendary in the South. Winston was a champion in Ben's heart, the best dog he ever owned. This book is a portrait of that special dog, and a living document of what the hunter's life spent bird hunting is in its purest form.

To paraphrase Ortega y Gasset, man molds a dog's style into the convenience of collaboration, something Ben has done with diligence and success for half a century longer than many of the readers of this book have been alive. The brief, finite moments that dogs grace our lives are as rewarding and fragile as a marriage. The commitments are similar.

This book will take you to all the places Ben and his friend Winston hunted. Together, they traveled thousands of miles by car and plane, hundreds of miles on foot—day after day of brilliant unspoiled time spent far from the incursion of man's madness into their lives. Ben's immersion into style of hunting and his approach to writing follows an adage that has stuck with me since I first heard it: Love the dogs before loving the hunt; love the hunt for the dogs.

Guy de la Valdene
Author of F*or a Handful of Feathers*
and *Making Game: An Essay on Woodcock*

Foreword

Unless you're independently wealthy—in terms of money and time—you have to make some hard choices on the journey of your hunting life. Relatively speaking, I made such choices early on.

Many of my adolescent and teenage hours were spent listening to the howl of basset hounds hot on the trail of pheasants. Short-legged, slow-moving, keen-nosed bassets make superb pheasant dogs. The only drawback is that they prefer rabbits to birds, and there was never a shortage of bunnies to divert the dogs' attention away from the more glamorous and gaudy ringnecks.

My family ate more rabbit pie than pheasant baked in cream of mushroom soup.

When I went out on my own, the responsibility of training and maintaining a hunting dog didn't fit into the picture. I turned to deer and other big game, as well as turkeys when they started making their big comeback a couple decades ago.

Ruffed grouse became a pleasant diversion when I planted roots in Minnesota, which was and still is one of

the best ruff places going. I could hunt the birds effec-
tively — albeit without grace or style — sans dog.

I was perfectly happy with the journey my hunting
life was taking. Until Ben Williams came along.

Working on a book about America's game birds, I
needed somebody to author a chapter on hunting
Hungarian partridge. Somehow I got the name of this
dog man from Montana who, it was put, was "nuts
about Huns." Ben accepted the assignment with what I
would soon learn was his typical energy, enthusiasm, and
good cheer.

We struck up a friendship over the phone as we
worked together and, as hunters do, ended up just "talking hunting" a lot. Not surprisingly, much of the talk
was about the dogs Ben owned and loved.

Ben had pictures for the book too. He sent a smat-
tering—80 (yes 80) gorgeous photos strong—of just
Hun hunting. He sent hundreds and hundreds of other
pictures too… of hunting every game bird in North
America, in all the spectacular landscapes the various
birds call home.

There was one constant across all the images. Nine
times out of ten the dogs in the photos were Brittanys:
strapping, handsome, mostly-white dogs with a little bit
of liver or orange on the ears and around the eyes, with
maybe a splotch or two of color on each flank, like somebody dropped a little bucket of paint there.

When Ben invited me to hunt with him for a
few days, I of course accepted. His enthusiasm was
undeniable. The hunting sounded fun. I had become

hooked on the idea of chasing those Huns in the
starkly beautiful landscapes I had known only as an
antelope and mule deer hunter. At the time the dog
work seemed secondary.

The hunting was beautiful.

There was the allure of the land—country so big it
felt mighty free to be out there in the middle of it all. It
was Ben's home ground: Oceans of grass and sage that
rolled, buckled, twisted, and folded their way up onto
the flanks of snow-capped mountain ranges with names
like the Crazies and the Absarokas.

Then there were the birds: Huns of course, but also
sharptails. It was easy to get excited about new game,
especially birds as hardy and ruggedly beautiful as the
land upon which they lived.

But the dogs were most beautiful of all. Ben owns
thirteen Brittanys, plus two English pointers. We
would hunt a foursome at a time. They coursed
through cover like restless ships on a golden and rolling
sea, disappearing below a swell and then popping
up on the crest of another wave, returning to the
mother vessel occasionally to check in. Then they
would cast back out again in search of an elusive
treasure of bird scent.

When they found that scent and locked up on point,
the excitement for me was almost unbearable. Walking
past the statue-like dogs for the flush was intense
enough. Keeping up with a battery of crouching, creeping, pointing Brittanys as they tried to relocate some
wild-running birds was even more thrilling, culminating

in a rush of wings and a symphony of *chrrrk chrrrks* as the partridge finally flew.

Only later did I realize that the hunting wasn't so much about the Huns. They were revered, of course, but the essence of what happened out there was about the dogs. The relationship. The companionship. The hunting partnership.

Ben Williams wasn't so "nuts about Huns," although he truly loves and respects the birds. Rather, Ben is even more nutty about his Brittanys. Huns were the wonderful tool that brought him and his dogs together.

I saw the pride in Ben's eyes when the dogs did well —which was almost all the time. I saw the same fire in the dog's eyes. They knew their role, loved it, and loped proudly and elegantly across the waves of the land as they did exactly what they were born to do: find and point birds.

I asked Ben a couple of times which dog was his favorite. He could never really choose. It was usually whichever foursome was on the ground at the time. He loves all his dogs and always has something good to say about each one.

So I asked the question in a different way. "What if your life depended on one dog, one strip of cover, and having that dog find and point the lone bird there, then retrieve it after you shoot it. Which dog would you take?"

"Winston," was the answer. I thought he meant the Winston on the ground. But looking back, I am quite sure he meant the original Winston, father of the present

Winston and the subject of this book, *Winston: The Life of a Bird Dog*.

I heard a story or two about the original Winston. And I thought he must have been quite a dog—to have a son named after him, perhaps in hopes that with the name would come similar hunting and pointing skills. It seemed to have worked.

But with so many hard-hunting Brittanys in front of us in the wonderful now, stories from the past didn't seem pressing.

That's why, when Ben told me he was writing a book about the first Winston, I couldn't wait to absorb the words. I had found Ben's prose as clear, eloquent, and descriptive as his pictures, when he wrote about Huns for my upland birds book. He did the same in the telling of these fourteen stories.

Simply enough, that is what you will find here: Some great hunting stories. This is not a sentimental collection designed to make you cry your eyes out for a long-lost pup. Rather, they're just great hunting yarns spun around the life of the best bird dog a man ever owned. Along the way, you'll learn a lot about dogs and game birds too… as well as gain insights into the characters who add so much color to our hunting pursuits.

We all long for a few good hunting stories now and then. This is such a collection.

I wish I could have known Winston and hunted behind him, if only for an afternoon, up there in the sage and golden grass on the flanks of the snow-capped mountains. He hunted many exciting birds in far-flung places, as you will read. But I'm also sure he loved his home ground the most, and thought that the wild Huns he was familiar with provided a perfectly fine snootful of scent.

But, because I am a lucky man indeed, I can in a way hunt with Winston: see him point, look into his eyes at the end of the day to see what knowledge they hold. Because a part of him is curled at my feet right now. Her name is Scout, and she is his granddaughter. Colored like him, and proud and strong already, there is a wisdom in her hazel puppy eyes that I can't under-stand... and an intelligence that is different than ours, but grand indeed.

Yes, my life's hunting journey has changed course. And I feel all the better for it. I can thank Ben Williams for that.

There is a new and different fire inside me, a happy new companion at my side, many exciting adventures ahead. Although Scout will cruise the popple woods and tag alder swamps more than she will the almost endless Western fields her grandfather loved, and prob-ably won't be quite as well-travelled as her progenitor, that won't make any difference to her. Every day afield is a celebration.

And that, I hope, is what you take away from this book. It is, simply and purely, a celebration of days afield and of a magnificent dog's life.

Winston seems like the perfect name for a dog that did so much, so well, in his hunting life. The name sounds regal, strong, and proud. I'm sure that's what he looked like, cruising the cover and then locking up on a bird or covey ahead, waiting for his master to come flush the birds and knock one out of the air to be retrieved.

In fact, I'm sure that's what he's doing right now.

Tom Carpenter
Outdoor Writer
Editor, North American Hunting Club Books

Introduction

Some bird hunters say a man only deserves one great dog in a lifetime, and great pointing dogs certainly do not come along too often. But with my Brittanys I was able to start with good bloodlines on both sides of the family tree, which allowed me to develop a line of hardy, intelligent, big-running pointing dogs. Through fifty-odd years of keeping a kennel full of high-performance Britts, I've had more than my share of great dogs.

McGillicuddy, Leo, Daisy, Shoe, and Chantilly were all good gun dogs through those early years. And, at present, my males Mac and Hershey carry on that tradition. I've owned well over a hundred pointing dogs over the years, but Winston, one of Shoe's sons, was the most outstanding bird dog I ever had.

Winston covered thousands of miles over the years, and together we hunted places so remote that no other canine, other than a few Arctic wolves, left tracks in the same soft earth. Together we chased birds in parched desert moonscapes, wet rain forest, open grassland prairie, sagebrush flats, steep talus slopes, golden stubble

Winston was from a long line of high-performing Brittanys, but from an early age he stood out as something special.

fields, uncut standing corn, and overgrown woodlots. We traveled by train, boat, car, pickup truck, and aircrafts large and small, in search of every species of North American upland game bird in its respective habitat.

I readily admit to having a bias toward my line of Brittanys. I try not to play favorites among individual dogs—although Winston was just that, a favorite. But Winston got 'em all and at a young age. So this book is a celebration of some of our wonderful hunts and our many travels together.

Ben O. Williams
June 10, 2003

Home

Chantilly's third litter (all sired by my male Shoe) whelped eight pups in the winter of 1988, and like their parents, the pups were predominantly white with orange ears. All were spoken for long before Chantilly had even been bred. I reserved first pick, and a hunting partner of mine had second choice. He called to ask if I would pick his pup for him and keep it an extra month because he would be out of the country on a fishing trip. I agreed, happy that it would give me more time to make a final selection between the two pups.

A month passed and I was still undecided as to which male to keep. Both dogs showed equal hunting potential and looked almost identical. In fact, every pup in that litter turned out to be an excellent hunter.

My purpose as a breeder of Brittanys has always been to have outstanding bird dogs for my own use—and to enhance the quality of the breed for hunting in open country. Breeding for monetary gain has never entered into my thinking. I ensure that each pup in my bloodline goes to a good home and is used as a hunting dog.

The day my hunting partner arrived to pick up his pup, one was helping me shovel snow and the other was dragging around my old red wool shirt. Picking a great pup out of a litter usually requires about as much skill as pulling the lever on a slot machine. It's really more luck than ability when they are that age. Good bloodlines are the most important factor; pick the parents, not the pup.

So maybe I just got lucky, but I chose the pup dragging the wool shirt. (Although my hunting partner claims that he is the one that got lucky.) Over the years both male Brittanys turned out to be fine hunting companions.

I named my new pup Winston.

As a pup, Winston disliked being alone in his kennel run. Even though I had twelve other dogs in the kennel, he still felt lonely. If I worked outdoors I usually let him out to be with me.

It wasn't long after the other pup left that Winston developed a serious lung infection. After three days at the veterinarian's, my wife Bobbie brought him home and nursed him back to good health. From then on, of course, he became our permanent housedog. But being a house pup also gets lonely, so I took him with me to work or run errands whenever possible. There were situations where he had to be left behind, though, so Winston spent short periods with the kennel dogs—but he never liked it.

It's astonishing how quickly a pup fits into a household. Once Winston was over his illness, he learned in a matter of days to "woof" to be let outdoors. At night, Winston slept in his dog nest next to my bed. He never whimpered or barked. But if I got up, no matter where I went, he'd follow me. If I poured a glass of juice from the refrigerator he'd be in the kitchen. If I read a book in the living room he'd lay down next to me. Even at a young age, though, Winston had an aloofness about him, and he never demanded attention. Yet he seemed to know that I liked him close by.

At the time Winston came along, I was retired from teaching and working at home. To this day, all of my professional writing and photography is connected to bird hunting, bird dogs, and bird guns. I usually write during the winter and spring so I can arrange my schedule around hunting and training my dogs. It so happened that Winston was the only dog I had to train that year.

All of my other dogs were experienced, fully-trained hunters, so working with them was usually just a matter of exercising them in the field. Whenever I exercised the kennel dogs I brought Winston along, too. And even as a little fellow, the other dogs liked him and treated him with respect.

During the colder months, I'd take several breaks from writing each day so that Winston and I could play together in the snow or in the woods.

He loved having sticks thrown for him. He'd chew them playfully while running in a circle, hoping I'd give chase. Periodically, I'd clean up the woods around my place, and he'd drag large branches around, thinking he was helping. Whenever I walked the perimeter of the property, Winston crisscrossed the meadow, digging holes and looking for critters, but he also kept an eye on me.

I have a routine I use on every dog I train, and Winston was no exception, even though he was my housedog. My kennel dogs are fed in the kennel area. My procedure goes like this. Twice a day all the dogs and pups are exercised together under my supervision in a large two-acre enclosure. I clean the kennels, give the dogs fresh water, and prepare their food while they are exercising. There are two dogs to a kennel run and they are fed together, with a dish for each dog. I fed Winston at this time, too, keeping him close to the other dogs. I always stay and watch all the dogs eat.

This procedure is important. All the dogs know they get to exercise and then come in and eat. This makes it easy to call them in. They have a routine and look forward to being fed. Within a week of starting Winston on this routine, he was completely trained to come when called.

I also took Winston with me in my vehicle whenever possible. At first, as some pups do, he got a little carsick. To overcome this, I started by only taking him on short trips, such as to get the newspaper at the end of our gravel road or to drop off refuse. I'd put him in the front seat with his head on my lap, crack open the window, and let him look out and smell the cool air.

As he became accustomed to the motion, I began to take him on longer trips to the store, to get the mail, to

Young Winston showed early on that he had a good nose and energy level.

Within six months, Winston was on his way to becoming a good bird dog who loved to hunt the massive prairies outside my home.

get gas, and so on. Pups are just like kids; they love to go wherever you go. I've always believed that pups that aren't exposed to the outside world may become terrified of new surroundings and may take more time to train in the field.

When Winston was five months old I took him fly-fishing with me. He had no idea what I was doing, of course. When I waded into the river, he did the same. But with the water so deep and Winston so small, he had to swim back and forth from me to shore. After a while, he just sat on shore and howled. To stop him from crying, I found a spot where I could wade only ankle deep so he could be close by.

When I hooked that first trout in front of him, Winston saw the fish splashing and ran out to fetch it. He couldn't catch the small fish in the water, but once I beached it, he tried to retrieve it. The trout kept slipping out of his mouth and I yelled for him to stop because I didn't want the barbless hook to catch in his mouth, but he kept trying to pick up the fish. I finally rescued the little trout and put it back in the water. When the fish swam off, Winston followed its wake.

After I went back to fishing, Winston waded out belly deep, put his head under water, and looked for fish. I'm sure he thought he was helping me. No matter what I ever did, Winston thought he should be involved.

When he was three months old I took him out with the other twelve dogs for field-running sessions. We trained in the cool heat of morning. I worked two braces of dogs at a time and ran them at least an hour. As summer progressed and the green hillsides turned golden-brown, I extended the training sessions past midday.

Conditioning dogs in the heat of the day is important preparation for successful early season hunting in hot weather. As with any athlete, conditioning is the key to success. At first, I ran Winston for short periods with each new group of dogs. This gave him a chance to know all the dogs and exercise three times a day instead of just once.

Several times while working in high cover he lost sight of his surroundings. Unsure of himself, Winston sat down and howled for me to find him. Once found, though, he would bound out to look for the others dogs again.

By midsummer Winston had become extremely independent, but not competitive. He honored his kennelmates and never broke point until the birds flushed. I felt Winston was well on his way to becoming a good bird dog. It was now time to take him out alone to find birds.

Burnt Tree

Any serious ruffed grouse hunter has many coverts where he knows birds will be during the next hunting season if the grouse population holds. The same is true with prairie game birds. As long as the habitat has not changed drastically, a new generation of game birds will fill that space. The number of birds may be greater or smaller depending on the weather, but they will be there.

In the West, in open prairie country, words such as "cover" or "covert" aren't really used. So I name Hungarian (gray) partridge coveys after familiar landmarks or associate them with how they were first found. The Burnt Tree covey is one of them.

During my years studying, hunting, and working pointing dogs on the prairie, I fell in love with the partridge. I welcome the hot and cold days, constant wind, snowfall, Chinooks, blizzards. I enjoy working young, inexperienced dogs and older, wiser dogs throughout the seasons, finding new generations of gray partridge each year. It is always a special occasion to see new green life appear under old golden clumps of grass or to see a pair of grays flushing underfoot from a dog on point in sight of the "burnt tree."

I started hunting the Burnt Tree covey long before Winston was born. The shortgrass prairie that surrounds the burnt tree has remained the same through the years. Only the moving clouds rearrange the landscape. Every spring, I flush at least one pair of birds near that old lonesome pine. And with each flush I confirm that a covey of grays will be in the meadow for the dogs to find in the fall.

I first found the Burnt Tree covey long after the prairie-scorching fire that scarred the tree had passed through. The flames had cut deeply into the grassy leeward side of the limber pine. A rock outcropping had saved its windward side. Over time, the smooth, light-gray bark worked its way back around the fire's scar, leaving just a few deep annual growth rings visible.

I first learned about the covey through a ranching friend named Peck. I had known him less than a year at that time and had permission to park my vehicle in his ranch yard and walk his land from there. In the early sixties, Peck's posted signs read, "Hunting on Foot Only."

On the day I learned about the covey, two Brittanys, Gina and McGillicuddy, Winston's great-great grandparents, were in the back seat of my "bug," a blue Volkswagen. Peck was standing in the opening of a big tool shed as I pulled into the yard. I'm sure he had heard me coming. I stepped out of the car, and we shook hands.

We kicked a little dirt, talking about the weather, how much grass the cattle had, and bird hunting (in that order). With ranchers, you talk about important things first then move on to what you are really there for. I asked if he had seen any Hungarian partridge.

Peck thought a while, then slowly started drawing lines in the dirt with his foot, talking quietly.

"Moving heifers to their winter range a bunch of those little chickens—You call 'em Huns don't ya?— spooked my horse. Lost my hat and darn near fell out of the saddle. You're welcome to hunt 'em.

"You'll find them up on top," he said, pointing his finger to a distant mountain. "You can't miss it. There's a lone tree, a big pine, burnt during a prairie fire when my dad first bought the place."

Pointing back to the lines in the dirt, Peck continued, "That's three miles from here. Follow the dirt road through two gates and stop by the salt lick. You can drive, so the dogs won't have such a long walk back to the rig when you're done hunting." That was Peck's way of giving me permission to drive on his place.

The first gate opened easily, but on the second one I started to wish that I had someone else along to help close it. After driving through, I wrapped my body around the fencepost and with both hands managed to pull the wire loop over the top to secure it. Once the gate was closed, my first thought was that I would have to do this again on the way out.

I parked the Volkswagen on bare ground close to the salt lick. The black earth, packed down by the heifers, glistened in the hot sun. The two dogs didn't wait for me to get my side-by-side 20-gauge out of the backseat. They jumped out and headed for the creek. I filled a metal pan half full of water and placed it in the shade beside the hunting rig and then called the dogs back. After numerous calls, both dogs came in, their muzzles and bellies dripping with muddy water. They flopped down to drink from the pan.

I refilled it so they would have water when we got back, put on my vest, and started uphill. The parched bluestem grass crunched underfoot as I walked across the prairie. (Where I live in Montana, early September can be hot and dry, with no rain for several weeks at a time.) The dogs worked both sides of the dry creekbed. I followed the cattle trail to the top. I could see quaking aspens at the far end of the long canyon, their leaves shimmering against the cobalt blue sky. From the lines Peck had drawn in the dirt, I guessed that the lone tree was still a good distance ahead.

The Brittanys hunted the grassy hillsides of the canyon and flushed a covey of partridge that went over the top. At this time, I did not know the lay of the land and had no idea where the birds had gone. I figured I'd look for them later after we searched for the Burnt Tree covey.

The dogs found a water seep under the quakies, and we stopped for a rest. I sat on a large rock, looking at the lone pine still a half-mile away across the golden field of grass.

I covered the half-mile while the dogs continued working the rolling prairie. At midafternoon we finally reached the burnt tree, but found no birds. The dogs and I relaxed under the pine. I gave them the last of the water I was carrying, ate an apple, and examined the exposed annual rings of the tree, trying to discern its age. It's difficult to judge a tree by height alone in this rocky, dry, windswept, shortgrass prairie country, and I guessed that the pine was over a hundred years old. Even the exposed annual rings had probably grown long before the first pair of partridge nested in the large open meadow below the tree.

McGillie dug holes in the rocky soil, trying to find cool dirt to lie down in. Gina waited impatiently to get moving again. Sitting there, I tried to envision the wildfire that had swept across the meadow, engulfing the solitary tree.

A soft breeze moved the grass; it had a feeling of moisture. Both dogs caught the air movement, and the three of us were on our feet again, walking into the wind in search of birds.

 Gina found them first while working a low swale about a hundred yards beyond the burnt tree. I came over a low hill just as she clamped down. McGillie honored her point from fifty feet away. As I moved up, so did he. I walked past Gina, and for a moment time seemed to stand still under the wide blue sky. The dogs broke. There was a burst of wings, and I raised the shotgun to my shoulder, following the whole covey with my eyes. Finally, picking out a single, I fired. It could have been an easy double (if there is such a thing), but I watched the rest of the covey fly off as McGillie retrieved the downed bird.

We moved in the direction of the flush and within fifty yards each dog found and pointed a single. I managed to kill three birds, and that seemed like enough. As we walked back toward the burnt tree the dogs found another single, but I didn't shoot. The sun was starting its descent, and I hoped the covey of gray partridge would get back together before the western horizon put on its beautiful nightly show.

By the time the three of us got back to the car, the bright colors had left the sky. The two dogs finished the water left in the pan. I was glad Peck had let me drive in, for we were tired. Opening the difficult gate on the way back was worth the trouble though.

These days, I sometimes drive to the upper meadow within sight of the burnt tree, but most of the time I prefer to park beyond the second gate and walk through the beautiful canyon, listening to the quakies sing of the coming of winter. The "Hunting on Foot Only" signs are gone. "No Hunting or Trespassing" signs have taken their place. Evidently, the change had something to do with antelope hunters. Now all the gates are locked, but Peck gave me a key some years ago.

I try not to hunt the prairie covey more than two or three times a season. Some years, the covey has only a few birds, probably due to a poor spring hatch. But most years the birds number between fourteen and twenty. Each year, I shoot only the surplus, leaving plenty of stock going into the winter. In excellent years, the burnt tree area can have more than one covey, but everything has to be just right: good carryover cover, a mild winter, several pairs of birds in spring, and most important, an ideal hatch with plenty of insects for the chicks.

I love training pups in the area around the burnt tree. Maybe it's because I have a sentimental attachment to the birds and the beautiful landscape in which they live. Like its Eurasian ancestors, the Hungarian partridge is still a bird of the temperate grassland ecosystem. The unmarred prairie plateau that I hunt is much like the birds' native home, the steppe country of central and western Asia. Here I can walk for miles and miles across land where the marks of man's intrusion aren't visible.

I'd been looking forward to spring in Winston's first year so I could run the six-month-old pup in the shadow of the burnt tree. Year in and year out this is one of my most dependable coveys. I figured these birds would offer the ideal training opportunity for Winston to discover his hunting instincts.

By March, most of the snow had melted and been consumed by the ground. This is breakup time for the coveys, a time when paired-up Huns are unafraid of human or animal activity. They hold like glue for a pointing dog. This is the best time of year to train a dog on Huns. When a dog goes on point, even if it's too close, the birds still hold. The male usually flushes first, and many times the dog can relocate and point the hen. This doubles the steepness of the learning curve, giving a dog two solid points on a single pair of birds. The birds are mature at this time of year, and they give off lots of scent. After the snow melts, the moist ground also improves scenting conditions.

I stopped off at the ranch house to visit with Peck and to show off Winston. By now, Peck had become a good friend, and with each new pup I raised, he wanted a blow-by-blow description of how it performed in the field. Peck has never hunted and knows nothing about pointing dogs, but he loves dogs. He has two small Pekingese that he takes everywhere he goes. Both dogs ride with him no matter what he is driving, be it a tractor, Jeep, or three-wheeler.

After sharing a couple of cups of coffee, I was on my way. Winston was in the passenger seat next to me, nose pressed against the window. Up the steep hill we went, Winston sure he was in charge.

As I bumped along, I was thinking I should probably change the name of the Burnt Tree covey to Peck's covey. For each time I hunt them, I'm reminded of Peck's drawing in the dirt.

I parked beyond the second gate and walked up through the canyon. The quakies were bare and silent that early in the year. Not even a bud showed. Winston sniffed the gray-haired droppings of a coyote, then trotted off on last year's cow trail. This was Winston's first time alone in the field, and he seemed unsure of himself, stopping to look around for the other dogs.

I departed from the main stem of the canyon and turned into a draw that leads to the grassland plateau above me. A blast on the whistle and Winston was on his way back to me. He realized I was turning and bolted ahead at full speed. Isolated patches of snow still covered the lee side of the draw. I followed Winston as he crisscrossed the ground a hundred yards ahead of me. Several times he stopped to make sure I was coming, then he bounded off again, hunting into the wind. The draw flattens toward the top, and the walking became easier.

On top, the large rolling grassland plateau appears level, but I knew better, for it has many folds within its landscape. The old burnt tree came into view, still a long way off. Winston started to feel more comfortable. He stretched out farther and farther, gaining confidence as he went. Periodically, he circled behind me before setting off briskly on another cast

The afternoon light had softened and warmed the native grass. A mellow glow swept across the rolling plains. Winston disappeared out of sight downslope. For several minutes he was lost from view. I hurried my pace to look into the depression. Not far from where the land falls away, I saw him make game, scenting the cover. He moved slowly, as the cover ahead was birdy, then he stopped. Head high, he pointed rock solid. I walked slowly beside him. "Easy, easy," I cautioned quietly.

He never moved, just rolled his eyes at me and looked back at the short cover. Nothing moved on the ground, but when I took two more steps a single Hun flushed in my face. Winston broke and ran in and out of the cover, soon flushing the second bird. He stopped and pointed after the flush, looking a bit embarrassed.

"Good dog, good pup, good pup," I said, but he was too busy scenting the cover to hear me. I finally got his attention, and he came back for a pat on the head before tearing off in the direction the two birds took. Just fifty yards out, he pointed again. He remained motionless as I moved up to pass him.

"Whoa," I cautioned as I kicked the cover, anticipating the whirr of wings.

It did not come.

I kicked again. Nothing.

Winston never moved. I called him up, and he pointed again, ten yards in front of me. This time I walked briskly by him and two Huns flushed just yards ahead. Winston raced past me in hot pursuit. I laughed, letting him go. You have to let a pup have a little fun. In time he would learn that chasing is of no use.

I have raised and trained a good many bird dogs, but each time a new pup makes its first point I get a lump in my throat. I have often wondered what goes through a dog's mind when it points, but I know that it is probably just reacting with the genes its ancestors gave it.

I was ecstatic. Winston had made his first point in sight of the old familiar tree. "Winston," I said, "We'll be back in the fall to hunt in the shadow of the burnt tree."

I was glad the light was on in Peck's kitchen as I drove up to the ranch yard. I had to tell someone the good news. Rarely do I bring a dog into Peck's house. Not that he cares, but his two Pekingese put up such a fuss that it isn't worth it. But this time was special. I was so proud of young Winston that I had to show him off to Peck, who met me at the door.

"Peck, remember years ago when you told me about a covey of birds by the old burnt pine tree? Well, today my little pup Winston found them on his own." On and on I went, giving Peck a full description of the day's hunt.

Watching Winston make his first point at Burnt Tree was exciting, and a moment I will never forget.

I apologized for bringing Winston in with me, but Peck seemed pleased, saying, "You can bring that new pup of yours in anytime. My dogs seem to like him."

After Winston's first point, he began finding his share of birds when out with the other dogs. As the hunting season approached, he seemed to be drawn to birds like a magnet.

No only did Winston steal my heart during those early days, he seemed destined to become a great dog. At eight months, he was performing much like his father, Shoe, who was still in his prime and top dog in my kennel of Brittanys.

Winston became a big, strong-running male with muscles of steel. He seemed to float across whatever terrain he was hunting. Chasing rabbits and other furry critters was not part of his teenage agenda, nor did he bother with rattlesnakes or porcupines. He knew I wasn't interested in them so he wasn't either. He never looked fatigued, even after long days afield. I'd return bone-tired to the hunting rig at the end of the day, and he'd make one last cast, often finding and pointing yet another bunch of birds.

Some people would rather their dog be a hunting machine than a hunting companion. Although he was only nine months old, I was lucky enough to find both in Winston.

I felt he was ready for the opening day of bird season. So when Buck called to ask if I would like to start the season early, I took him up on it.

Northern Lights

For most of us in the lower forty-eight, Alaska is usually seen as the most desirable region in which to hunt and fish, yet one of the most difficult in which to live. Folks have known this since the days of Seward's Folly in 1867, when Alaska was purchased from Russia at a price of two cents per acre. In mild weather, it can seem like an outdoorsman's Valhalla, but during foul weather it becomes inhospitable, to say the least.

Today, hunting and fishing in Alaska usually means traveling by small aircraft to and from an isolated makeshift camp or an outback cabin. And ptarmigan hunting is no exception. It's still a challenge. I'm not talking about a dangerous or life-threatening challenge, but a challenge of being alone one hundred miles from civilization, of "walking the edge" with miles and miles of Arctic tundra underfoot.

In my mind, the "edge" is where the tundra begins and the forest ends, where the land opens and ptarmigan thrive. In late spring the rivers rage with snowmelt as permafrost loosens its grip on the endless spongy muskeg. As the temperature warms, this beautiful barren

landscape may show you a herd of caribou moving slowly under a forest of antlers, or a grizzly working the
shoreline of a small lake. It's not uncommon to see a
moose feeding on a small willow patch.

Yet by August the cranberries have already bright-
ened to a red glow and large flocks of white tundra geese
are passing overhead, their cackles warning that winter is
not far behind. Alaska has the earliest bird-hunting season in the United States—beginning at sunrise on
August 10, to be exact.

Choosing to bring nine-month-old Winston with
me when Buck called to invite me up to Alaska to hunt
ptarmigan didn't seem fair to all my more experienced
dogs, but as he was my only house dog, I guess it was
justifiable. The kennel dogs still had a long season ahead
of them, and I wouldn't let them down. So I took the
pup on his first trip down the hunter's road, bringing
along only his father, Shoe.

Looking out the window on the first leg of the flight,
I wondered if Winston was as frightened as his father.
Shoe never liked flying, and this was a Metro-liner cigar
tube that sounded like a buzz saw cutting a forty-inch
oak log. This was Winston's first trip and I can't imagine
he liked being in the dark belly of a noisy prop plane.

In the Seattle airport, I watched as both dog crates
were loaded onto the big 737 headed for Anchorage,
Alaska. I saw Shoe lying glued to the bottom of his crate.
Winston was looking through the wire door of his crate,
hoping for some attention from the attendant nearby.
The young woman rubbed his nose, and he wagged his

whole body. Then both crates were whisked onto the conveyor belt, disappearing into the black hole. That's the last I saw of them until they slid down the unloading ramp at the Dillingham, Alaska, airport.

The dogs braced themselves in their crates as they were loaded in the back of Buck's pickup along with my hunting gear. We bounced down a gravel road for a mile or so then turned right toward Buck's house.

"Where are we going to hunt?" I asked.

"On the edge," he said, "About an hour or so air time from here. We'll have a floatplane drop us off on the bank of a huge river not far from a shack we can use. The shack's not much, but it's better than a tent."

Driving along, Buck explained that willow ptarmigan were abundant that year. They'd be nearly everywhere in Alaska's high, treeless country. "Even though they are accessible by highway, the best hunting is still by bush plane," he noted. "Like many other Arctic creatures, the willow ptarmigan are starting to change from their summer plumage to their winter plumage. The fact is they also have another color phase in spring during the breeding season, and it's possible to shoot all three color phases because of Alaska's long hunting season. You should come back and give it a try in the spring."

I nodded in agreement. "You know, Buck, talking about color phases, the red grouse of Scotland, even though a different color, are similar to our willow ptarmigan of North America. British sportsmen lucky enough to shoot the highland moors recognize them as the king of game birds.

"At one time in the British Isles, opening day of grouse season was a national holiday, but that's an old tradition. Their shooting season opened on the so-called 'Glorious Twelfth' of August. Up here your hunting season starts two days earlier than theirs. Maybe they should declare 'The Glorious Tenth' a national holiday in Alaska."

Buck nodded his head, laughing.

The evening was cool for late August. I felt heavy moist air as I got out of the pickup at Buck's modest home. Shoe and Winston also seemed to sense the difference in the air. Winston lunged out of his crate with all of the enthusiasm a young Brittany can muster. Shoe was unsure of himself after the long trip and came out slowly.

Both dogs sniffed the air, staring into the dark spruce forest as if some foreign creature might be lurking nearby.

"It must be the moose they smell," Buck said.

I fed the dogs and put them in the garage attached to the house. After much talk about ptarmigan, we retired for the evening.

Morning came early. Low-hanging clouds clung to the tops of the dark-green spruce, but Buck assured me that we would leave on schedule. The area inland from Bristol Bay is famous throughout Alaska for fierce storms and continuous bad weather, but that day the weather was relatively warm; cloudy with a slight breeze of five knots or so. We flew beneath the cloud cover, running south then west a while, the pilot updating Buck on the weather as we went.

Looking out the window of the Cessna, it was easy

to see the Arctic desert sprawling to the curved horizon, its vistas unscarred by roads. The open tundra had countless ponds grooved by glaciers. Little vegetation appeared on its bleak surface, and there was no sign of life at that altitude.

The lakes and ponds shimmered under the pallid sunlight as we passed over. I was thinking about all the Arctic flora and fauna that has adapted to this vast wilderness domain. I wondered what the view was like in spring after the snowdrifts had disappeared and the tundra was ablaze with vivid greens and multicolored flowers.

But this was late August, and looking across the landscape I saw only the melancholy barrens. My eyes searched for ground movement. I wanted to see a grizzly bear or a long phalanx of caribou moving southward.

I felt fall waning as I scanned the country. And I was sure it wouldn't be long before the last platoon of geese passed overhead, the skies no longer echoing their lonely cries. After I'd be gone the first snows would come early and quickly cover the barrens, and the land would be clutched by winter. The ptarmigan would turn white, and silence would descend upon the tundra.

I turned to my partner, "One thing's sure, Buck. After flying over this country there seems to be an abundance of land to hunt. It looks to me like it's just a matter of finding a place to land."

"That's right. It looks good from up here, but finding a good body of water to land on with oats or a landing site for wheels is always a problem. We'll be landing on a big river, but it will have to be high tide when we do."

   Buck asked the pilot to make a pass over where we were going hunt. The Cessna banked low over the tundra, and we saw groups of white dots scattered over the countryside. Buck's pre-scouting for concentrations of willow ptarmigan paid off. The pilot put his thumb up, banked again, and turned toward the river to land.

   Just ahead, I saw an old shack close to the river. Buck explained that the shack belonged to a couple of caribou-hunting friends. The Cessna seemed to drift sideways over the choppy water before skidding to a stop. The tide had already started to move out, sucking the saltwater back to the sea and exposing a muddy bank. The beach was twenty yards wide and gaining ground quickly as the tide slipped out. Above the high bank, all that was visible of the shack was a rusty galvanized stovepipe leaning away from the strong prevailing winds of Bristol Bay.

   It was late afternoon when we unloaded the gear and supplies on the wet beach. Winston peered excitedly out of the open aircraft door while Shoe remained flat on the floor bug-eyed and trembling. After we unloaded, the pilot was in a hurry to leave, but before closing the sliding window of the Cessna, he called out, "Weather permitting, I'll be back in four days. Wednesday about ten in the morning." Full throttle, he lifted off, cutting into the chop on the water. Airborne, the plane turned 180 degrees and sliced through the dark, low-hanging clouds. Then all was silent.

   The cabin was on a high bluff about a hundred feet from the river. It was mostly surrounded by muskeg, with a willow and alder thicket on one side split by a deep little creek draining the interior. Its muddy water dumped into the big river, which was a highly-productive sockeye salmon fishery. Only a few remnant salmon carcasses lay along the mud bank. The brown bears and rainbow trout that follow the salmon runs were gone.

It was raining by the time we carried all the gear and food into the shack, and darkness was not far behind.

Sitting by the stove, I was thinking about all the ptarmigan I saw on the ground. Then I said to Buck: "This is Winston's first hunting season, and after seeing all those birds I wonder if he was my best choice for this trip. You know he's just pup. He's never seen that many birds at one time in his life. The fact is, Winston has never had a bird killed over him nor has he ever retrieved."

"You know," Buck answered, "these birds have never seen a human or a dog. Ptarmigan generally walk from danger rather than fly in this open habitat, and they're often visible to hunters and dogs. They have little fear of ground predators and can be approached very close before flying."

"Buck, from my experience with hunting ptarmigan I know that a well-trained pointer will respond favorably and adjust quickly to pin birds down. I don't think ptarmigan are any different for a pointing dog than young sharp-tailed grouse. In fact, I'm convinced ptarmigan leave a stronger scent than other grouse, or it could be that the tundra has so much moisture that scenting conditions are always favorable. As you just touched on, the only problem I've observed when using a pointing dog for Arctic grouse is that many times the birds are easy to see. There are some dogs that just can't handle seeing grouse walking slowly away or looking at them eyeball to eyeball.

"I know that Shoe will be excellent. On the other hand, Winston still sight points robins on the lawn but also backs other dogs beautifully. He's only a pup, but I have high hopes for him. I think he'll do just fine. He's a smart dog and learns quietly. We'll see, I guess.

"One thing's for sure, while we weren't able to hunt last week on 'The Glorious Tenth' of August, I believe this is still the best time of year for hunting ptarmigan with a pointing dog. The birds are too young and not very fast fliers during the first week. But we both know that as the season progresses, depending on the weather, the birds form larger and larger flocks and become difficult to approach. By mid-September they are nomadic and move erratically from place to place. I believe this is not so much due to a fear of being approached as it is just restlessness. Many times, a flock will get up and fly for no reason and land almost in the same place."

"Another good time to hunt ptarmigan with pointing dogs is late April. Both males and females are on their territorial grounds and behave much the same as they do right now," explained Buck.

The next morning came late, not only due to the dark sky, but also because it was comfortable to be in a warm sleeping bag listening to the rain on the tin roof. The dogs were lying next to the stove as Buck fixed a late breakfast. The aroma of bacon filled the hunting shack.

Shoe and Winston had already finished their morning meal when we sat down to ours. It had rained most of the night, and thick fog hung low over the river, but even when it was clear or when the river was at low tide you couldn't see the other side.

Buck and I reluctantly slipped into rain pants, pulled on rubber boots, and laced up gaiters. Slowly we became waterproof. The dogs went out the door first, then Buck. I turned off the stove, tucked the 20-gauge side-by-side under my rain jacket, and closed the door behind me.

A wet blanket seemed to cover the tundra. Although the rain had stopped momentarily, I could see more coming. Based on our flight over the hunting area, we both decided that the best ptarmigan hunting should be on the far side of the alder thicket.

I sent the dogs down through the heavy cover and watched them go out the other side and up the hill. Walking a path worn smooth by grizzly bears, I crossed an alder-lined creek and zigzagged through wet, spongy muskeg and worked my way up a gradual incline to a ridge. Once on top, I could see miles upon miles of unbroken wilderness. The vast, unmarked country sprawled to the curved horizon in every direction.

The dogs descended the gradual slope first. Below us, I could see white dots arranged in unfamiliar patterns on the scabrous, never-ending tundra. Then the little patches moved. As I looked out across the muskeg, there must have been hundreds of willow ptarmigan scattered around in small bunches.

The daily bag limit for ptarmigan was twenty birds, although I didn't plan to shoot that many. I'm sure hunting pressure has little effect on their yearly population. Each year the ptarmigan population is either feast or famine, and this year it looked like a feast.

Buck caught up to us after being sidetracked for some unknown reason. He said something about fresh grizzly tracks back by the alder thicket, but all I could focus on was the white dots. We quickly discussed how to approach them as we moved down the slope. Within a few minutes the white dots took the shape of birds.

A hundred yards ahead, Shoe and Winston saw and smelled the birds and locked up on point. Forty yards farther on, three ptarmigan nervously milled around in front of them. We slowly moved past the dogs. Both Brittanys relocated and pointed in front of us.

Winston got impatient and started creeping. I whispered to him in a low voice, "Whoa, Winston, whoa, whoa," but still he moved slowly ahead, putting one paw up then the other. "Whoa, Winston, whoa." Then he broke point and charged past Shoe, who stayed motionless. There was a whirr of white wings as the birds flushed—just beyond the range of our open-bore, 20-gauge shotguns.

I called Winston and he came back reluctantly. He knew exactly what he did wrong, and I scolded him. The pup turned his head and looked away. I pulled his ear softly and said, "No, no, no. Bad dog." After several seconds I patted him on the head and stroked his back. "Take it easy, boy." But he wanted to go, so I said, "OK,

Winston, you little varmint, let's go get 'em." He raced off full throttle looking for Shoe.

Buck laughed as he walked over. "You're sure tough on that pup, Ben."

I was laughing too. "Well, the little fellow did a good job under the circumstances. He hasn't even had time to stretch his muscles, then he runs right into three birds on the ground. That's the first time he's ever seen a bird on the ground other than a few robins.

"You know, Buck, I think one bird flushed sooner than the other two, and that's what caused him to break point. But that's still no excuse, he shouldn't have flushed the other birds. I'm sure he'll get the hang of it and do better next time."

"There are plenty of birds here, Ben, and this is a good place for a young dog to go to shooting school. I'm not into killing numbers, and I know you aren't either."

We walked over the soft muskeg toward another distant white patch of ptarmigan. Both dogs worked easily through the soft, wet cover. Storm clouds hung low over the tundra, and the distant hills were no longer visible. A soft, cold mist swept over the landscape, making the birds more difficult to see. Many of the white patches moved erratically from place to place for no apparent reason.

Buck and I stopped to watch the way the birds were moving. Neither of us was knowledgeable about ptarmigan habits when it rains, but we were aware that something had triggered their flighty behavior. I suggested that, like us, the birds may feel more threatened if their visibility is diminished. Buck nodded in agreement.

We sat on a carpet of reindeer moss, hoping the foul weather would pass. No such luck. After we rested for a while, the light mist turned into a steady, cold drizzle. Neither dog showed signs of being cold, but they were impatient to hunt so we move out, hoping the rain would stop.

Both Britts crossed a spongy muskeg swamp, then worked a slope covered by a large patch of cranberries. To my amazement, rock outcroppings broke the surface. The soft, spongy carpet became a little firmer for the first time since we left the shack. I felt like I was walking on air.

Suddenly Winston turned and pointed back toward a rocky opening. I looked in the direction he was pointing but saw nothing. Buck called out when he spotted Shoe high above Winston. He was locked up rock solid, but not honoring Winston's point. As rain and wind swept up the slope, we could see four birds looking nervously down at us from above Shoe. It was obvious the birds moved up the gradual slope when they saw us coming. We passed by both dogs, and neither moved a muscle. At fifteen yards, the birds started milling around, then sprung into the air. Both guns sounded off.

Winston raced to the closest downed bird, picked it up, then spit it out as he choked on the loose feathers. He grabbed it again and made his first-ever retrieve. He stood proudly in front of me but refused to give me the ptarmigan. By this time Shoe had retrieved one bird and had gone back for another.

"Winston, give me the bird!" He reluctantly let go

Winston was eager and excited as the Cessna landed in Alaska.

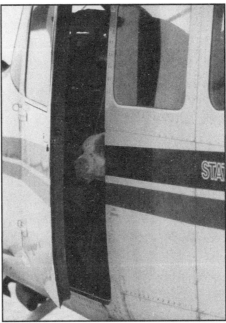

*Hunting ptarmigan all day on the tundra of Alaska was
exhilarating, beautiful, and tiring! The small shack was a
welcome comfort after our days in the field.*

and raced back to see if any more birds were down. After he searched the area I called him back, knowing there were no more birds on the ground. Then he was off again, running into the wind to find more birds.

It was still raining, but on the way back to the shack the dogs found five more bunches of birds. Both did an excellent job of pointing and/or honoring each other, which under such tough conditions amazed me.

Late afternoon faded gently away, and there was a softness about the tundra as we walked back. All four of us were wet and cold. It felt good to enter the dry shack, but a warm stove felt even better.

Blue smoke soon belched from the oil stove in the corner, making its way into the dark, misty sky. Drops of rain ran down the outside of the stovepipe, vaporizing before they hit the hot stove. Buck and I sat in makeshift chairs with our feet propped up in front of the stove and had a drink. Both dogs curled up under our legs as close to the stove as possible.

The weather improved little by the next day. Storm clouds still moved across the tundra, changing the colors of the landscape every few minutes. The rains came and went throughout the morning and each time the weather cleared, the birds behaved better and held for the dogs. Late in the afternoon, the sun suddenly burst through the clouds, and the tundra came alive with light and warmth.

Winston and Shoe pointed flock after flock of birds. Sometimes the groups numbered five or six, others upward of fifty or sixty birds. We hunted southward in the open, barren country, never losing sight of the dogs as they worked flocks of ptarmigan on the tundra. Some groups flushed wild, but neither dog gave chase. For Winston, retrieving birds became routine.

The light faded in early evening as heavy rain clouds built up off the coast. The birds were on the move again. We arrived at the shack with hearts pumping, legs sore, and vests full of ptarmigan. It felt good to get back. Buck hung the birds beside the weathered wooden door while I wiped down the wet, tired dogs. With so many birds to work, Winston had come into his own this day. My pup was everything I thought he would be.

In Alaska, you can feel and see winter coming. And as another day began, I felt it in my bones and saw it in the flighty, erratic patterns of the ptarmigan. It was a sure sign that Arctic winds would soon be funneling down. Small family groups had joined together and the huge flocks were as nervous as cattle being shipped to a slaughterhouse. Instead of shooting, Buck and I were content to watch the dogs maneuvering to hold the huge flocks. Sometimes they succeeded, sometimes not. As I walked along, I wondered if the dogs and I would ever see this number of grouse again in a single outing.

Early in the morning on the fourth day, strings of ptarmigan passed over the small shack, following the coastal river like migrating waterfowl. The weather looked unsettled, but the airplane arrived on time.

As we loaded up, the pilot said, "It's clear to our destination, but the chop on the water tells me to hurry."

And we did.

Steppe Grouse

So as a young pup, Winston had a head start before the usual hunting season began at home. He had the opportunity of a lifetime in hunting Alaskan ptarmigan, and it was certainly a marvelous experience. The good scenting conditions and plentiful birds gave young Winston a preseason edge in developing his inherited skills.

It's my belief that when a young dog with good genes is put on wild birds, it only takes a day or so for the light to click on. And that dog will retain its instinctive pointing skills the rest of its life. A dog's ability to retain such perfection is amazing.

You may have to shake out a few lose hairs each year, but Fido will be as good as ever. Once a dog has developed its instinctive pointing ability, it becomes like an old shoe that just needs a little polish now and then. The important point to remember is that daily conditioning, or at least regular exercise, before the hunting season starts, will allow a dog to perform to its full potential.

I call the grouse I hunt most often "steppe grouse," but most hunters won't recognize that name. Call them sharp-tailed grouse or sharptails, though, and most folks will know that you are talking about a bird of the open prairies. Today, the sharp-tailed grouse is the most abundant grouse on the plains. They occupy desirable habitat over a huge area of North America. Montana, the state in which I live, is particularly noteworthy for its fine sharp-tailed grouse hunting, and it's a great place to train young dogs.

On the opening day of bird season, the vegetation is still partly green. The red buffalo berries and dark purple chokecherries remain partially hidden by the green leaves that still cling to the trees. The wild currants and soon-to-be-ripe snowberries cover the sides of the sagebrush coulees.

Winston's first season was a banner year for wheat crops, and plenty of golden kernels were left under the high stubble. The last cutting of alfalfa was still in the fields, with bright blue blossoms standing knee high. Food and green vegetation were everywhere, and I was thinking it was going to be tough to zero in on where the birds would be.

Over the years I have been blessed with outstanding sharptail hunting. This year appeared to be no different. To me, there is nothing better for a young pointing dog than early season sharptails. The young birds are still in small family groups, and they hold their scent and lay tight for a pointing dog—the perfect combination for training a pup. They just go together. Before the season started, Winston had already found and pointed his share of young sharptails, but of course there were no birds to retrieve. That was about to change.

Winston was in top form for a pup, and my hope

was to get him into birds as soon as possible that morning, before scenting conditions diminished as the heat built. The rancher told us the birds had been in the alfalfa field every morning until he cut the big grainfield. He hadn't seen them since. "That was a week ago," he said.

I figured the grouse would be in the edge of the stubble or in the hayfield chasing grasshoppers that morning.

Lisa, my hunting partner that morning, sat patiently as I finished my coffee. I thanked Elmer, my ranching friend of many years, and asked if it would be okay to park by the haystack between the large cut wheatfield and the standing alfalfa.

"Have at it." he said. "If you get hot and need a drink or a bite to eat, stop back for lunch. You should have your birds by then."

The wheatfield stubble was cut higher than usual. I put a beeper collar on Winston, and Lisa put one on Sage, her male Brittany. I uncased my Browning 20-gauge over/under and she did the same.

I watered Winston and he was off. Sage was a little standoffish and didn't take a drink.

"Sage, drink," Lisa demanded. Sage looked at her and ran off after Winston.

Lisa is a wonderful hunting partner and has an outstanding dog. A friend gave it to her as a gift. She knew nothing about training a bird dog, but she loved the dog and wanted to be involved in the training process, so she quit her job to spend a year with a professional dog trainer.

Sage learned his lessons well. But once on her own, Lisa's discipline with the dog became a bit lackadaisical. In other words, she did not have full control of Sage in the field. He loved chasing furry critters. In fact, he loved to run deer out of the country, and he seldom returned until exhausted or until he lost sight of his quarry.

On one occasion, Sage disappeared over the farthest hill and became lost. Lisa called and called, but received no response. I suggested we go back to the pickup and drive the gravel roads to look for him. On our way, I met Elmer driving home.

"Elmer," I said, "We were hunting your place and Lisa lost her Brittany. His name is Sage. If you see him, would take him home and tie him up? He's a nice dog and will come when called. We'll check in with you in about an hour."

Elmer nodded his head slowly in agreement then looked over at Lisa. Smiling, he said, "Ben has hunted my place for many, many years and has never lost a dog." Within a half hour we found Sage running down the gravel road toward Elmer's ranch. He knew exactly where he had left us.

I stopped to tell Elmer we had found the dog and to thank him. Then Elmer said to Lisa, "Why don't you have Ben train your dog so it doesn't get lost." Lisa looked a bit embarrassed, but we all laughed.

With our guns out, we put on hunting vests and follow the two dogs.

"Lisa, the way I figure it, this hunt should be a slam-dunk, and like Elmer said, over by noon. But as you know, things don't always go as planned."

"Yes, Ben, the last time you said that, we didn't find birds until we had walked our legs off."

"Well, if you recall, it was hot, much like today. And hot weather with no wind will play tricks on a dog's nose. That's why I figured we'd get an early start."

We hunted down the first long golden strip, broad and a half-mile long. The sky was a pale blue, with no clouds in view. I estimated that by noon the temperature would be in the high eighties. After lunch we could hunt the cool forests for mountain grouse.

At the end of the field we called the dogs in for water. They were hot, and so were we. We crossed a fence, then a lane, and then another fence as we moved into an alfalfa field and headed back toward the pickup. Still no sign of birds.

The green alfalfa field was much cooler, still holding a little dew. In many parts of the arid West one or two cuttings of alfalfa is normal. But this year a third crop had started, although it was thin. The dogs could move freely through the sparse cover.

With heads held high to scent the dry air, the dogs disappeared, dropping out of sight over a low hill. The beepers were silent for a moment, then we heard the hawk scream that indicates the dogs were on point. We quickened our pace. I walked past Winston, then Sage. Both dogs relocated in front of me. I looked for movement in the tops of the pale blue flowers, gun held ready, waiting for wings to grab air.

The dogs moved in. Nothing. I looked over at Lisa and shrugged my shoulders just as a lone hen pheasant got up a hundred yards away.

It was obvious that sharptails had been using the field. Feathers or fresh droppings were on the ground each time the dogs got birdy. We crisscrossed the field several times, but the birds just weren't where they were supposed to be. Why the birds were absent puzzled me.

After a couple of hours we returned to the pickup and gave the dogs a drink of water. I sat on the tailgate, eating lunch and thinking about going after blue and ruffed grouse. Higher in the mountains it's much cooler during the middle of the day. Then it occurred to me that yesterday's weather was overcast and cool, with light rain.

"Lisa," I said, "I believe the feathers and droppings are from yesterday. And I'll bet the birds were feeding in the hay meadow midday after the rain. But today they probably fed earlier this morning, and we missed them."

Just then, Lisa looked up and pointed to a lone sharptail flying high over the pickup, headed for the sagebrush at beyond the wheatfields.

"There's a big coulee running through the sage at that's full of good lofting cover and that bird is flying high. I bet it's going to where the other birds are."

Her eyes sparkled. "Let's go get 'em," she said.

Lunch was delicious, but the break a short one. Lisa put Sage up to rest and I replaced him with Shoe. I activated the two beeper collars and we headed across the stubblefield in the direction of the lone grouse. The dogs were already out of sight and out of beeper range.

*Lisa hunted over her dog, Sage, and my dogs Winston and Shoe.
She bagged her first sharptail on this trip.*

Winston was becoming an excellent retriever.

After we crossed the big wheatfield, I turned to follow a grassy swale. Lisa didn't say anything, but I could read her thoughts. I'm sure she wanted to follow the sharptail she saw and not the swale. I knew the country and where the birds hang out though, and she didn't.

The grassy swale ended within a half-mile. The wind was at our backs, and I suggested we cross the open benchland at a right angle to the next swale. The tall, pale-golden wheatgrass glistened in the sunlight as long shadows started to form across the prairie. It was still hot for that time of year, but I could feel the late afternoon moisture coming on. The dogs also sensed the onset of the moist evening air and picked up their pace.

I explained to Lisa that walking to the head of the swale and crossing the grassy bench put us in a better position for hunting the draw to windward.

The sun was at our backs and a light breeze picked up. Lisa moved down the swale toward the deep draw and I followed, watching Winston work the heavy cover. But still nothing caught his keen nose.

Three hundred yards ahead, the draw became brushy with snowberries, rose hips, and sagebrush. Fifteen minutes had passed before Shoe and Winston got to the snowberry patch. Both dogs froze. Winston was ten feet ahead, motionless. Lisa quickened her pace, but I signaled her to slow down. Both dogs relocated and continued through the brush and up the side of the hill, but still nothing.

The sharptails had been there but were now gone. The hillsides steepened as we moved toward the canyon.

I called the dogs back, and Lisa dropped into step beside me as we headed back to the pickup. We talked for a while about where the birds should be.

I looked up the steep slope then toward the rig and suggested that the sharptails must be on the edge of the sage and the grassy bench.

"Lisa," I said, "the only time the dogs got birdy was when we first entered the draw two hundred yards back. The dogs moved up the hill, then quit."

Lisa twisted her ponytail and asked, "Do you think the birds flew?"

"Could be, but Shoe could have just lost the scent in the heavy sage. Our best bet is to go back above where Shoe got birdy and hunt between the sage and the bench. Let's go, time's running out."

"Yeah," she laughed. "What happened to our easy hunt!"

"Every time I say a sharptail hunt is in the bag, some unforeseen thing happens. That's Murphy's law."

Puffing, we hoofed it up the sidehill, following the edge of the sage. Both dogs worked downwind and not to their advantage.

Winston moved above and beyond the snowberry patch. The sage thinned at the edge and opened into a low, grassy, horseshoe-shaped depression.

Both dogs spun around windward twenty yards apart and froze.

"We found them," I said softly to Lisa. "Take your time. You go ahead, I'm going to concentrate on watching young Winston."

Lisa hesitated, not moving. She looked back and forth at the two dogs. "Go on," I said, "but slowly."

She moved past Winston. Then I walked next to Shoe. His head tilted slightly back, both eyes glued on the pale golden grass swaying rhythmically in the breeze.

The low sunlight had cast long shadows across the grass of the depression and turned the surrounding prairies a brilliant orange. "Darn it," I said to myself, "I wish we had long-billed caps and shooting glasses."

I stopped as Lisa took two steps past Winston. Several sharptails lifted above the tall grass, their shadows crossing the open prairie.

I fired at a single bird that cut away from the bright sun, and it fell at the edge of the swale.

Lisa hesitated with the first wave of birds, then both barrels sang out. A single bird fell, then silence. I watched as the birds disappeared, becoming small specks that I lost in the sun.

Winston retrieved a sharptail to me. Then Shoe did the same. I praised both dogs, and they were off running toward the blazing sun. I walked over and handed Lisa her beautiful sharptail.

Surprised, she looked at me, then at the bird. "The sun was blinding. I didn't think…"

"I know, but, yes, you did," I said. I shook her hand and she laughed.

Because it was still a warm day, I suggested that we gut the sharptails before getting to the rig.

"Ben," Lisa said, "if it's okay, I'd like to keep this

magnificent bird and show it to Sage. It's my first sharp-tail, and he has never seen one up close."

"That sounds fine, Lisa. The last time I saw the dogs, they were headed toward the birds and the setting sun. I know where they are. I used to get angry with Shoe when he disappeared over the horizon. Time after time I would lean on the whistle only to walk in the direction he took and see a small white speck motionless a quarter of a mile away."

As we walked back, the western horizon was ablaze with color. I pointed my finger and looked at Lisa; she saw them as well. Two white specks were motionless on the grassy slope we had previously crossed.

The dogs were not chasing the birds, but relocating, then pointing the sharptails again.

I walked over to Winston, and Lisa moved up on Shoe. Each dog had a single sharptail pinned down, and we each collected another bird. Then both dogs brought the birds to me.

Winston covered a lot of Montana prairie during his first hunting season. I didn't keep track of the number of sharptails he pointed. I wish I had, though, for it was a great number.

Peck's Place

The ranch house lies in the shadow of a row of prairie willow, trees that were planted long ago when the homestead was new. A muddy little cottonwood-lined creek runs below the house. I often stop in at the house to see Peck when I hunt his place, even though I have a standing invitation to go when and where I like. The time of day I visit depends on both of our schedules. I know Peck's routine and he knows mine.

As I mentioned earlier, it took a year before Peck gave me permission to drive the backcountry on his ranch, and he knows I respect his grasslands and drive only on the designated two-rut roads. "Vehicles leave tracks," he said, "you can see them for years."

Peck himself never drives any vehicle cross-country on his land. The only places I park are beside the salt licks used for cattle. That's where most of the two-rut roads lead, and they usually have a place for a vehicle to turn around. The rest of the land is wild and pristine.

I walk Peck's place more than he does, but he knows every blade of grass and respects his holding more than any rancher I've known. He is a steward of the land, never overgrazing any section of his property. If you were to view his property from a small aircraft you would easily be able to identify his property lines by the amount of grass he has compared to his neighbors. That's why Peck's place is Hun and sharp-tailed grouse heaven.

Peck's ranch is a working ranch, and his house is of modest means. The living room is full of well-worn furniture. At one end is an open fireplace, going full blast if the weather is cold. Occasionally, he and I sit in the reclining chairs in the living room and talk. But most times when I stop in we sit in the kitchen on chairs made from old steel tractor seats sprayed John Deere yellow and green.

Peck's house smells of breakfast, lunch, or supper, depending on when I arrive. If he is in a talkative mood, he offers me something to drink, but never the choice of beverage. It may be coffee, iced tea, or after I hunt, wine, beer, or hard liquor. I rarely refuse because this is his way of asking me to stay longer. If Peck seeks more conversation, he refills the cup or glass before you have a chance to refuse.

I was late this morning, so I didn't stop to see if he was home. Hopefully, I'd have another chance when the hunting day was over. I drove the rutted lane across the rolling plains toward Sheep Mountain. It took most of a half hour to get there.

The first barbed-wire gate was open, but I had to stop to open the second. The September dust rolled past the pickup as I drove through and stopped. The gate closed easily behind me. I bounced down the dusty two-track for another mile until I come to the salt lick.

The six dogs in the compartments over the back of the pickup knew this was the place I was going to hunt. I stepped out, and the dogs started clamoring in anticipation. Cattle had packed down the ground around the salt lick, and their trails lead into the golden western wheatgrass, which danced in the cool wind.

I released the dogs. They raced to the creek for a drink and came back dripping with mud. The creek was almost dry, so I put fresh water down before putting three dogs back into their kennel boxes. Winston put up a fuss as I forced him back. He howled a sad song long after the beeper collars of Mac, Leo, and Pattington were no longer audible.

The dogs found the first covey of Huns within a half-mile of the rig while running the sidehill along the creekbed. All three caught the scent and stopped. I saw four or five Huns darting around in the sparse grassy cover. As the birds ran to heavier cover, Mac moved first, then froze. The other two dogs backed Mac, but never budged.

I walked slowly past them and two young birds flushed almost in my face. The 20-gauge over/under seemed to respond on its own. Sometimes it's just too easy. I held up, not taking the second shot. The remainder of the covey followed the creek toward the end of the canyon.

I knew where those birds were going, so I made a mental note to save them for Winston later in the day.

The dogs found two more coveys, one as we circled back to let the other dogs out.

I shot another bird, but lost sight of the covey as I exited a chokecherry patch. Huns are quick to use a landform to block your view of them. Anyway, shooting a brace was enough for these older dogs, so I decided not to follow them.

Winston greeted me with a series of howls when I returned to the rig for lunch. I watered the tired dogs, put them up, and let my spoiled pup out. He took off at a dead run, but I called him back and made him stay close while I ate an apple. I scratched behind his ears, and he rubbed against my leg. He didn't really want affection, though, so I let him get a drink from the pan on the ground.

I called him back again and held him long enough to finish my apple. I wondered what was going through his mind. Hunting is demanding for a bird dog and I'm sure he wanted to please me, but his hunting instincts took over and he wanted to be out there on his own. Dog and man need each other, and when hunting together there has to be camaraderie between the two.

I gave him a hug, and then he was gone.

I let the other two dogs out as well. While putting on their collars, I gave them some attention, but they were also in a hurry to get going.

With three fresh dogs on the ground, I prepared to head out again. In my mind, the lay of the land is anchored by at least two coveys of Huns that I named years ago. Year in and year out the Cedar Post covey is easier to find than the Twin Gate covey, but it also depends on the amount of cover each year. This year, the cover was excellent and the birds numerous.

While running a fenceline, Winston found birds, and Shoe and Tilly backed. I thought it was the Twin Gate covey, but as I walked in, two sharptails jumped and feathered the wind. They took me by surprise, and my first shot was rushed; the second hit its mark. After the shots, Winston broke, flushing and scattering the rest of the flock.

Shoe got to the downed bird first. After the retrieve, I released the sharptail from his mouth and he was off again, running in the direction the birds took. I called Winston back, and he looked a little sheepish when I told him to "hunt dead." He found the bird I placed at my feet, picked it up, and then dropped it, choking and spitting out feathers. The next instant, he pounced on the sharptail again and then sat down.

"Good dog, Winston," I said, "but before you follow the birds, you rascal, make sure to hunt dead first." I took the bird from him and he was off again in a happy mood.

The day before he had remained steady to wing when a large flock of sharp-tailed grouse thundered skyward one by one from a patch of snowberries. He realized that more birds were still on the ground, so he stayed put. When the last grouse lifted off, he broke point and seemed proud to retrieve.

But this day he had run right through them, not waiting for the rest of the flock to get up. I didn't scold him because I really didn't know if he had done anything wrong. Poor scenting conditions could have confused him into thinking the birds had left, or there could have been some other factor not readily apparent.

"Let the dog be a dog," I reminded myself. He was only a pup. And pups need to have fun, too. When hunting the grasslands, my pointers learn to be steady to wing only if part of the covey flushes. If the dogs remain rigid after a flush, I know more birds are present. All of my dogs learn this, but if they do break it's not a big deal to me. I believe they learn to remain on point from being cautious as young dogs sight pointing robins and rabbits in the yard.

And, yes, some of my dogs point bunnies in the field now and then. I don't care; they're just having a little fun. But I never shoot rabbits. If they got the idea that I wanted to bring home rabbits, they would seek out every bunny hideout in the country.

I also don't want my pointing dogs to remain steady to wing after all the birds have gone. I want them to key in on flying birds and to get the downed birds as soon as possible. Huns run when wounded, and the dog has to get to the bird quickly. Why lose time in finding a downed bird?

When a covey is flushed, everything goes into motion: shooters, dogs, and birds. Why should the dogs stay rigid? They should have as much fun as the gunner. There's nothing wrong with the chase—if it's controlled.

I actually want my dogs to follow a covey after all the birds flush. I'm not talking about chasing birds, but rather locating the covey again and then pointing. I used to get angry with my dogs for doing this, but not anymore. Invariably, I find them pointing the covey I previously flushed, so now I just let them do their job.

I saw Shoe and Tilly frozen in mid-stride as they continued working along the fenceline, still within a hundred yards of the sharptail flush. I wasn't sure which dog pointed first. They looked like a set of bookends placed six feet apart. Winston came up from behind, saw the two Brittanys, and immediately backed, forming a perfect triangle.

I was wondering again if we had found the Twin Gate covey. The covey flushed in unison, and all three dogs broke in the direction of the birds. I refrained from shooting so I can watch Winston's reaction to the birds.

The covey turned sharply, flew over the top of a hill, and dropped out of sight. The dogs followed but then returned to check out the area where the Huns flushed.

Sure of where the birds were headed, I climbed the hill toward the Twin Gate covey. The dogs were out in front, searching all the likely cover where I've found these birds before. Nothing. Winston got birdy once, but still nothing happened. It occurred to me that the birds may have quickly flushed again, not liking the spot where they landed.

I shook my head and smiled. There have been times when I honestly thought I had this covey figured out. But Huns can still fool man and dog much of the time, for they know their living rooms better than we do.

On the way back to the hunting rig, Shoe and Tilly

each found a single sharptail, part of the flock that Winston scattered earlier.

I put the two older dogs back in their kennel boxes so I could hunt Winston alone. My plan was to go after the covey first flushed by the other dogs; the ones I marked down earlier. I was sure it was just a matter of time before Winston found them. By now the birds had laid down plenty of scent, and I was fairly certain of where these birds landed. Winston drank plenty of water before we left.

I walked a little less than half a mile up a hill and down the other side, then dropped into a canyon and followed the creek. I've hunted this covey for years and almost know them by their first names.

Winston was following the creek much too closely and needed to break out into more open country. I hit the whistle and back he came. I gave him a hand signal, and he turned away from the creek, moving along a golden sidehill.

Following a draw that rises out of the creek, Winston started making game. I was sure the birds were running up the draw ahead of him. I took off at a half-trot, knowing this was not in my best interest. But it was my pup and I wanted to see him work up close. Anyway, I thought, the birds were young and the season early so maybe my hurried steps wouldn't flush them prematurely.

The draw narrowed and the sides became steep. Winston slowed to a walk, then moved uphill into the wind. Above him was a large patch of chokecherries. The young dog stopped, then moved within ten feet of the

Brittanys in their dog boxes on the back of the pickup (above), and Winston peeking out to see what was going on.

*Winston delivers
a downed Hun.*

heavy cover. A single Hun flushed from the far side of the clump of brush. "Darn it," I said to myself. Then Winston froze. With head high, he inhaled the strong scent, his jaws vibrating.

I slowed down, huffing a little up the slope. Finally I got to Winston. Still breathing hard, I stopped to rest so I would be able to shoot better. Winston never moved, but he leaned forward, tense and trembling. Heart pounding and shotgun ready, I looked into the chokecherry patch. The understory was fairly sparse, and I could see ten to twelve Huns milling around not wanting to fly.

Winston saw them too, and his eyes rolled a look at me. "Winston," I whispered, "we've got to move up closer."

I almost think he nodded in agreement. I eased up several steps and stopped, but Winston did not move. The Huns walked a bit farther up the slope, still under the canopy of cover.

Waiting for the birds to flush, I looked over the chokecherry bushes and spotted movement. A dark shape materialized from out of the clouds, becoming larger and larger. Within a second, a prairie falcon screamed down the slope and skimmed the ridgetop. The sleek bird kicked in its afterburner and made a big loop, returning again low over the chokecherry cover. The Huns flattened on the ground and never moved. Winston never moved either, but I'm sure he heard the falcon screaming by.

A light breeze broke the silence, rustling the remaining leaves and berries that protected the birds from overhead danger. I was in a dilemma. Pup was on point, birds refused to fly, and I didn't want to flush the young Huns for the prairie falcon.

Unlike many hunters and dog trainers, I don't believe that you have to flush the birds every time a dog goes on point. Nor do I need to kill a bird every time for my own satisfaction or for my dog to retrieve. I was sure Winston understood my thinking. We'd both be back when the birds were older.

So I broke open my shotgun, took Winston by the collar, and led him down the draw. Within seconds he was running into the wind, with miles of open prairie to hunt. The gray falcon made several more passes as we worked our way back to the pickup, still hoping we'd flush a bird for him.

After hunting until the light started to fade, I stopped to see Peck. It was Sunday and cold for that time of year. I found Peck in a talkative mood. He'd had no visitors lately; I could see it in his eyes.

Before I had a chance to sit down, Peck asked about the dogs. "Is young Winston with you?"

"Yes, he is."

"Bring him in, it's getting cold outside."

So I sat in the yellow tractor seat in the kitchen, Winston pulling on his lead, trying to touch noses with Peck's Pekingese. I held him between my legs and gently said "No."

"Ben, would you care for a drink?" Same routine.

"Thanks. I would."

Walking to the freezer he got two frosted glasses.

"You look like you could use a cold one," he said. He went into the bedroom and came back with the glasses full of cold beer.

Up to this time, he had never offered me beer in a glass. After taking several sips, I mentioned that it was very good.

Peck looked at me and said, "It should be, it's draft beer."

I didn't say a word to question why he had cold draft beer in his bedroom, because with Peck you never ask why. You just wait for him to tell you. I slowly sipped my beer.

Then Peck said, "Aren't you going to ask me about the draft beer?"

"Well, I was, but I thought better of it."

Peck gave me a half grin and said, "Years ago I built a small, insulated shed against the outside wall of the bedroom to hang meat. I don't use it for that anymore, so I installed a keg of beer and piped it through the wall into the bedroom. That was the closest place to bring it into house. And it works great."

"Well, Peck, that's a great idea."

He took my glass, went back into the bedroom, and returned with a refill. Fortunately, I was able to get out of there after my second glass.

I hunt Peck's place often, sometimes once or twice a week, because the ranch is so big and I'm the only one allowed to hunt birds on the place. Most of the time I try to stop by to see him in the morning before I go hunting.

I hadn't been able to see Peck in the afternoon again for about a month after we'd shared our last beer. When I finally had a chance to, he offered me another beer, which I accepted.

This time, he went to the refrigerator and brought me a can of Bud. I thanked him and took a sip. Peck looked at me for some time, then started to talk.

"I suppose you would like to know about not having draft beer this time."

"No, Peck, this Bud is fine," I said, knowing he'd tell me about it if he wanted to.

"Well, I'll tell you anyway. After the third keg of draft beer went down the gravel road, most of the neighbors figured out it was being delivered to me. So they started coming to see me more often.

"The fact is, some of these folks had never set foot in my house before. And they're the ones who started coming every day. So I had to put a stop to it."

Thunder Chickens

For years I hunted wild turkeys and other upland birds in eastern Montana. I stayed with a friend who owns a large ranch close to the places I hunt. After supper one evening, our talk drifted from turkey hunting to sage grouse. Like most ranchers in that part of the country, Bert lumped all species of grouse together, calling them prairie chickens or just chickens.

"When I was a young boy back in the forties," Bert said, "my father and I used to see all kinds of chickens. We'd shoot the young ones, and Mother would fix them for supper. While going to feed the cattle, the birds were so plentiful we'd chase them off the road."

After a long pause, he continued, "Don't know what happened to them. Just don't see 'em anymore. Coyotes and foxes probably got them."

The reference to predation got my hackles up a bit. So I laid the limiting factor theory on him, which I had learned from a conservation class back in my college days. Or maybe it was from Aldo Leopold's book, *Game Management*.

"You know, Bert, we've beaten that dead horse

enough. The passing of the passenger pigeon was due to the bird's inability to adjust its habits to changing habitat conditions. The same is true with sage grouse. The bird is locked into a single plant ecosystem, and sagebrush grassland is shrinking at an alarming rate. Over the years, the long-term forecast has not been good for sage grouse.

"Historically, sage grouse inhabited all of the shrubgrass prairies of the West. Sage grouse were losing ground well before you were born and have continued ever since, even though numbers have fluctuated some years. In the early years, the decline of the big grouse was not well documented due to the lack of biological studies. But today it is.

"Bert, without sagebrush this grouse cannot survive. It needs this habitat year-round. Within this shrub grassland community the birds' range in spring, summer, fall, and winter is quite different. If you remove one of these habitat communities, the birds decrease in population or, in some cases, vanish. For instance, wintering areas that sage grouse inhabit usually include tall sagebrush in at country. These are also the first areas to be utilized by man, either turned over by plow or used extensively for wintering cattle.

"Thousands of acres of shrub grasslands have been broken up and interspersed with agricultural land. Overall, it doesn't appear to be harmful to sage grouse. But less birds can occupy this fragmented space.

"I know of several isolated flocks of sage grouse that were once plentiful. I don't shoot them, but I doubt this helps the population in the area. It's keeping the habitat intact that matters. If the habitat is restored in these places, the isolated flocks will have a better chance to multiply."

"Well, do you think these birds should still be hunted?" Bert asked.

"You know, when a game species declines two culprits are always blamed; one is man, the hunter, and the other is natural predators. Closing or regulating the number of birds harvested in a given year is beneficial if the numbers are drastically declining in areas, but it is not the answer to restoring the sage grouse population to what it once was.

"Although sage grouse had a dim forecast in the past, there is a brighter future ahead. State and federal wildlife agencies are working hard to restore some of the habitat that is still suitable for the birds' survival.

"Maybe today these big bombers should be hunted as trophy animals like mountain sheep are. I still pursue them. The dogs love it, and I don't have to shoot them to enjoy the experience. I highly recommend it."

Bert knows the history of sage grouse as well as I do. He just wanted to hear me talk.

He walked to the stove and got the coffee pot. Holding the pot above my cup, he said, "Refill?"

"No, Bert, I'll pass. I won't be able to sleep if I do."

He poured himself a cup, cleared his throat, and took a thumbnail scoop of Copenhagen. "What's the story about your dog Winston hunting his first chicken?"

"Well, call them what you want, but to Lyle they were 'thunder chickens.'"

Bert leaned back in his chair and waited. He's heard this story before, but he likes Winston stories as much as I like telling them.

"Seeing a hundred sage grouse in the meadow was not unusual when driving to Lyle Landson's ranch. The unimproved road to the ranch house and out buildings divides the hay meadow. Lyle told me that every morning and early evening the birds poured into the alfalfa to feed on the new growth after the second cutting.

"'It seems every thunder chicken in the county uses the field to feed,' he said. Laughing, he described the flocks as squadrons of fighter planes landing and then being hooked on the at deck of an aircraft carrier. 'When they hit the ground the birds come to a complete stop and almost fall over on their heads.'

"I presumed sage grouse were locked into a single ecosystem, but it never occurred to me that they had any association with alfalfa. Knowing that the birds relished this lush green legume plant was extremely helpful when hunting.

"That year's moisture proved helpful to the young birds, and the population exploded. The weather in June was unlike most springs in Montana. Thunderstorms formed every day over the mountains, dumping sheets of rain across the landscape of Joe Little Basin.

"As summer progressed I did manage to get out with my Brittanys and share some field time during the late evenings before the bird season opened. The dogs were a bit neglected because of all the rain. Their stamina could have been better, but their enthusiasm made up for it.

"Lyle's country is rugged, strong, and unforgiving. It lies in the shadow of clouds that form over the Missouri Breaks. Strong winds and thunderstorms roll across the landscape, appearing and disappearing unexpectedly like the thunder chickens themselves. Those few of us who hunted them regularly recognize that these magnificent birds and the land they occupy hold a magic that's indescribable.

"Fred, my hunting partner, drove slowly down Lyle Landson's lane toward the ranch house. We paid little attention to the vehicle as it followed the ruts in the dirt road on its own; we were too busy watching for sage grouse.

"Landson's hay meadow lay silent, and frost covered the tops of the tallest alfalfa plants. As long as I've known Lyle, he's never gotten a third cutting of alfalfa off the place because of the short growing season. By opening day of grouse season, the hay field was already dry. His third crop of alfalfa was void of tall plants, and most of the field looked like it had been cut with a lawn mower.

"A few grouse close to the dirt road flew farther into the field as we approached, others stayed and looked up as we passed by. Small family groups were scattered throughout the alfalfa field. Several big adult males flew off toward the sage flats, nervous about the hunting rig cutting though their feeding area. Still others never stopped feeding as the pickup crawled along.

"Fred stopped the vehicle to avoid hitting three young sage hens standing in the middle of the lane. They walked slowly off the shoulder of the road. The birds hardly moved when he stomped on the accelerator. This time of year, sage grouse have little concern for equipment, men, or dogs.

"By the time we got to house, Lyle's pickup was gone and the only thing moving around the buildings was his old cow dog. She greeted us with a quick bark, then a long slow *woofff, woofff.* My six Brittanys couldn't see out of their kennel compartments, but answered with a cheerful response.

"We passed more buildings and bounced down the half road, half cattle path for two hundred yards until it dipped into a draw that leads to Rustle's Creek. Fred turned left, the brakes squealing as we descended the steep, rutted, rocky incline down to the edge of the creek.

"Both Fred and I sipped coffee while getting our hunting gear on. Next guns came out, then two of my Brittanys, Winston and Mac. The big, benchland hay meadow was out of sight, but still loomed above us. The dogs were already far ahead as we walked diagonally up the steep grade toward the fence that separates the meadow from the sagebrush drainage. High above, gnarled juniper fenceposts appeared like sentinels guarding the horizon.

"My idea was to get to the edge of the hay meadow without any birds seeing us. We climbed to the top and stopped to catch our breaths. We rested a moment, then spotted the dogs' heads. Winston was out in front, but both dogs were motionless. Whether he pointed the birds first or stole the point I'll never know.

"I unloaded my 20-gauge over/under, dropping the shells while crawling over the fence. I got hooked on a barb, tearing my new hunting shirt.

"I said to Fred, 'Darn it, when you're in a hurry, things always get screwed up.' I held Fred's gun and he rolled under the barbed-wire fence without any trouble.

"Like stones in a field, the two Britts never moved. Eight young sage grouse stood at the edge of the open meadow watching the dogs. Once the birds spotted us they become uneasy. Both Fred and I froze.

"Thirty yards in front of us the land dipped into a grassy sagebrush gully, which stopped abruptly at the edge of the hayfield. The gully was not wide, maybe forty yards across and full of high sagebrush and tumbleweed.

"Slowly, the sage grouse disappeared into the gully. Fred moved first, walking past Mac then Winston. I did the same. Both dogs relocated, then stood rigid at the edge of the high sage cover. We followed, stopping to look into the gully. I hesitated, ready to take a few more steps, but the silence was broken by the loud clap of wings on air, and wave after wave of sage grouse filled the sky. It was over in a second. Four birds lay dead on the ground. Neither Fred nor I shot again; four was enough. Still other birds got up while the two dogs went after the downed birds. 'Sometimes it's too easy to kill these birds,' I said to Fred.

"This was Winston's first big sage grouse. A six-pound bird can be heavy for a young dog, and both Fred and I laughed as Winston struggled to make the retrieve. He picked the bird up and dropped it several times.

Finally, he managed to bring the big full-grown male over to me. By this time Shoe had retrieved the other three birds.

"After collecting the birds, we followed the same route back down the sagebrush slope. Not far from the pickup we sat down, dangling our feet over a cutbank above the creek. Both of us lay back on the grassy carpet to warm our faces in the sun. Our conversation turned to what birds we'd hunt the rest of the day.

"'What should it be?'" I asked Fred. 'Ruffs and blues in the mountains or Huns and sharptails in the valley?'

"He was about to answer when a tremendous roar of wings came from the direction of the meadow. A huge flock of sage grouse thundered overhead and landed on the far side of the creek.

"'Fred,' I shouted, 'I've never seen that many prairie game birds in the air at one time in my life! Have you? There must have been well over a hundred!'

"With a smile, Fred nodded his head in agreement. 'Let's go find some blues, the dogs haven't had a good workout yet.'

"Some time ago, Lyle got too old to manage the place himself. His children had little interest in the ranch, so the family sold the holdings and he moved to town.

"Whenever I drive through the small town were Lyle now lives, I stop to see him for a few minutes. Both of us rattle on about this and that. When I leave, he always walks with me to my pickup. Before I get in the hunting rig, we stand around kicking a little dirt and talking

Winston is happy after retrieving this beautiful sage grouse.

about all the good times. And he still asks about Winston, knowing how much I love that dog.

"It wasn't many years after Lyle left the ranch that the large numbers of sage grouse declined. Miles of wheatfields now surround the old homestead, and the hay meadow is gone. Not long ago, I drove past where the hay once flourished. Winston was much older then, and a new blacktop highway had been cut through Joe Little Basin. Today, both Lyle and the thunder chickens are gone.

"Bert, there are still lots of good places to hunt sage grouse. It is well worth the effort, and it takes you into lonely country. Sage country is like the bird itself: big, wide, and handsome. The sight of twenty or thirty large black-and-white prairie bombers catapulting into the sky all at once and feathering the wind gets your attention.

"Just seeing the 'Cock of the Plains' airborne is a memorable experience, whether you kill one or not. Every season, I like to work dogs in The Big Open. Just knowing there may be sage grouse in the area is intriguing. When thunder chickens flush they make shadows on the prairie. Winston loved to hunt them, and we did it often."

Bud's Birds

The sign on to the barbed-wire fence says "No Trespassing," but the gate is open. I park the pickup off to the side, clear of the muddy road. I toy with the idea of closing the gate, but then think otherwise; someone must be in the forest. Winston is out before I have my gear ready. He runs through the open gate, heading into the thick alder- and aspen-covered creek.

There are still a few cattle milling about, but not for long. It won't be many more days before the high pasture of blue grama grass is covered with snow.

Gray-green sagebrush hugs the steep slopes down to the aspen line between the mountains. At most, the rocky floor is only a hundred feet wide, with a small creek murmuring through it. Bud comes off the steep incline, herding two yearlings.

My side-by-side is still broken open on the tailgate when the two yearlings thunder through the gate, with Bud not far behind. I'm putting on my hunting vest when he arrives.

"Hi, Ben, looking for grouse?"

"Hello, Bud, nice horse. Have you seen any blues?"

Bud nods, looking at the top of the mountain then back at me. "The blue grouse are on the ridge. I saw them yesterday while looking for stray yearlings."

"Have you seen any ruffed grouse lately?"

"Same place as always. Along the creek in the aspen groves."

Bud's red heeler checks out my hunting rig, whizzing on both front tires.

"Red get back here," Bud shouts. "I better get going and catch up to those two heifers. Red's not doing his job. He's more interested in your huntin' rig than working cattle."

"Thanks, Bud," I say, and smile as he passes.

At the foot of South Fork Creek I start picking my way upslope following a cow trail. Halfway to the top the dog's bell falls silent, and I wonder if Winston is pointing or just out of earshot. I scan the steep slope for the dog when I hear a bird flush and the sound of the bell in the opposite direction from where I'm walking. Must have flushed a ruffed grouse, I think to myself.

Winston comes running from behind me, trying to look like nothing happened.

"Winston did you flush that bird?" I ask as he goes on by. "You slow down in this heavy cover," I shout, but the bell drowns out my voice.

Another bird flushes far below, but this time the sound of the bell is above me. The bird is a ruffed grouse, and I watch it sail to the bottom of the canyon, landing in a grove of aspen. I mark the bird down, thinking I will hunt the creek bottom on the way out.

Still on top, I enter an alpine meadow. I'm hoping this is the ridge where Bud saw the birds the other day. I can hear the bell off to my left, but can't see Winston. Then all is silent. Walking in the direction where I last heard the bell I scan the meadow. No dog, no sound. After walking several minutes I've gained more elevation. On the far side of the meadow I spot a white object standing motionless against the tall dark evergreens and bright blue sky.

As I approach, Winston comes clearly into view just below the ridge. He's standing on a large rock outcropping. Walking to the crest of the hill, I peer over and see that Winston is eye to eye with several blue grouse below.

One bird watches me as I move down the slope. The others continue to feed. Trying to keep my composure and balance, I ease down. Beneath my feet, loose rocks roll down the incline, breaking the silence. Suddenly the hillside erupts with the sounds of whirling wings, the deep-throated bell, and the loud report of my 20-gauge. An echo chases the birds and dog down the canyon. I call Winston back, and let him know there's nothing to retrieve.

Finding blues the rest of the day becomes easy. Winston finds and points three more bunches in the grassy meadows. My shooting improves. I kill a bird from each bunch, though I probably could have caught them with a net. Today, the blue grouse are everywhere in the high open parks.

I come off the mountain with three blues bulging in my vest. Winston has saved me many steps with his fine retrieves.

I follow an old cow path along the South Fork back toward the pickup truck. By late afternoon the sunlight disappears in the valley. To the left and right mountains lift high and the valley narrows. The wind is never so still that the quakies stay motionless, and every now and then I can hear the rustle of the shimmering yellow leaves over the sound of the dog's bell.

Walking along, I hear the murmuring creek. I sit on a log and watch the clear water racing down on its long journey to the sea. Steep hills hump up at my back. Today they are covered in sage; maybe tomorrow they'll be white with snow.

I call to Winston, who's not too far ahead. The bell falls silent as he sits next to me. He puts his nose in the pouch of my vest and pulls on the wing of a blue grouse. "No, Winston," I say softly. Then the bell sounds, and he's off again.

Walking again, I cross a small shallow depression and several frogs leap into the mossy seep. Within minutes Winston's bell stops. He's locked up on the edge of a grassy glade in a small clearing. Before I pass him a pair of ruffed grouse bolt for heavy cover. I hurry the first shot, missing the lead bird, but center the second before it disappears in a stand of alders. I call "Hunt deaaad, hunt deaaaad," but Winston, like a pro, is already retrieving the bird.

I continue hunting for Winston's sake. Four is plenty, even though five mountain grouse is the current limit. It's midafternoon when I come to a patch of chokecherry not far from the hunting rig. The last of the dark red berries are being eaten by migrating robins. "There are always ruffed grouse in this patch," I say to myself.

I call to Winston, and motion him to hunt the cover. For several minutes I hear the bell through the dry leaves underneath the chokecherries. Then silence. I walk to the edge of the high cover and look in. Winston is on the far side about twenty feet away, looking toward me. I see nothing on the ground.

There is a moment of pure stillness, no bell, no breeze. There's no way I can get through the cover.

"Let's go, Winston," I command.

But he stands motionless. I push my shoulder against the tall brush and hear a clatter of wings above my head. Two ruffed grouse burst straight up through the chokecherries. Instinctively, I bring the gun to my shoulder. Then another bird flushes skyward. There aren't many times when you have the advantage while hunting ruffs, and Winston has made a perfect point, but still I don't shoot.

It starts to cool down before I get to the rig. Three blues and a ruff is a fine bag for a day of hunting mountain grouse. The wind picks up and sweeps across the meadow. I close the wire gate and get into the pickup.

On the drive home my mind drifts toward spruce grouse, the other western mountain grouse.

Spruce grouse live in primitive country. Even today, there are still many unmolested miles of backwoods and high mountain forests in North America that are not often visited. The boreal forest in which spruce grouse

*Hunting the high mountain forest for spruce grouse (above), and
Winston taking a rest after a difficult retrieve (below).*

thrive is a moist environment; if not actually wet, it's usually locked in ice or buried in snow.

These birds are often referred to as "fool hens" due to their tame nature. They live a solitary life and are reluctant to fly when approached by man. But like all game birds, they should only be shot on the wing. And when pursued in this manner, they can make a fool out of you.

Winston's first spruce grouse hunt came on a soggy day on Alaska's Kenai Peninsula. Clouds crept in the same day I arrived and it poured rain all night.

When I hit the woods in the morning, the trail smelled of wet, rotting leaves and green spruce. I attempted to get off the trail, but after entering the woods, I had second thoughts. It was tough going, but Winston finally started making a few casts in the thick timber. Each time he returned to the trail, he looped in back of me. I suspected he was following my scent, not wanting to get lost.

Lunchtime passed without our seeing a bird. I back-tracked down the same trail, and Winston started running a little bigger. Every so often I stopped and listened for his beeper to make sure it was in the running mode.

I took a different trail and entered an area that was more open. Winston returned and ran past me. Twenty yards ahead, he cut off the trail and within seconds the beeper sounded the pointing mode.

I had to climb over deadfalls to get to Winston, and I was wondering if there really were birds there. Then I saw them. One was on a log, and two more were feeding on red berries. Finding an open shooting lane would be difficult, but I was glad he'd found the birds, even if I missed.

As I moved forward, Winston trembled but held firm, watching the grouse walk back and forth on the log. I stepped over a tangle of underbrush and stumbled, flushing Mr. Spruce Grouse straight over my head. The other two birds flushed moments later. I got a quick shot off, but didn't cut a feather.

It was late when Winston eventually found a pair of grouse out in the open. One bird flushed, and he stayed steady after the shot. The bird fell dead at the edge of the timber. The other bird flushed a second later, going to heavy cover before I could shoot. Winston retrieved the downed bird, and we called it a day.

Gravel Roads and Good Folks

Most years, I spend a few days in South Dakota and Nebraska in mid-September. Not because the bird hunting is better, but just to enjoy new places on the face of the landscape, to visit with old friends, meet new folks, and work my gun dogs on prairie chickens. To get there from Montana, I drive country roads instead of the interstate. Traveling secondary or county highways is not the fastest way to get from point A to point B when going on a hunting trip, but it's my way of doing it.

By the time I took that year's trip, Winston had miles of field work under his collar. And after his first trip hunting ptarmigan, I had never left him behind when I took to the hunter's road.

A few years earlier I had met a farmer who lived not far from the White River in South Dakota. As a young man, he hunted a lot on the national grasslands and on many private land holdings from Pierre, South Dakota, to the border of Nebraska.

"If you ever want to shoot some chickens [prairie chicken] and grouse [sharp-tailed grouse]," he told me, "you can go to my son's place where I used to live."

So I gave him a call. "Hello, John. Ben Williams speaking."

"Good to hear from you, Ben. Are you coming this way?"

"Yeah," I replied, "I have a new dog by the name of Winston. I need to get him into some prairie chickens."

"I'll call my son and tell him you're coming."

"Do you want to hunt with me?" I asked John. "I'll be coming alone with five or six dogs, and I'd like you to see two-year-old Winston hunt. He's a dandy, maybe the best dog I've ever had."

"With all those good dogs of yours, that's saying something. Stop by my place and stay overnight. And if I can't go, my son may."

"Well, John, you're welcome to. How are the birds this year?"

"I've seen four or five flocks that feed in the alfalfa field in the morning and spend the rest of the day in the hills."

"Chickens or grouse?" I asked.

"This year, mostly chickens. They seem to be coming back in good numbers, but not like when my father was a boy."

"Good," I answered, "I'm looking for prairie chickens."

Dust rolled past the pickup truck as I came to an abrupt stop in the blocked roadway. The only things visible from behind the flatbed wagon were two bulging round hay bales, and they were taking up most of the narrow, washboard road. A rancher crawled out from under the large hay wagon, which was being pulled by a big green tractor. I surprised him as I pulled slowly alongside the wagon.

"Do you need any help?" I asked.

"No thanks," he said. "Just checking the axles. If you're traveling this road you must not be in a hurry. How many dogs are you carrying in that hunting rig?"

"Only five this time. How's the rest of the road to the blacktop highway?" I inquired.

"Like a boulevard if you go slow enough," he said laughing. "I see by your license plate you're from Montana. Where are you headed?"

"To hunt prairie chickens with a friend, and then on to Nebraska to do some grouse hunting in the Sand Hills."

"That's a long haul from here. You're the first vehicle I've seen this week and maybe the last before winter sets in," he laughed again. "Why did you choose this route?"

"I don't like traveling expressways. I can look over more potential bird-hunting country by sticking to gravel roads," I explained.

"If you come back this way, stop in and hunt my place. It's down the road a piece. Seems like a good year for birds," he said, smiling.

I nodded my head. "Thanks. I just may do that."

I pulled slowly away, kicking up dust. Looking back, I saw him climbing into the cab of the John Deere. "Friendly folks in this part of the world," I thought to myself. I'd like to stop and hunt his place on the way back, but this time, like most trips, I won't

have much wiggle room for extra hunting days on the
way home.

Miles down the road, the Rohm ranch came into
view. I've known the family for many years. When I
returned, my plan was to hunt a day with Marvin, the
youngest member of the family, but right then my destination was farther east.

I drove all day to meet John by suppertime. After we
ate and fed the dogs, I brought Winston into the house.
We sat by the wood stove in two old rocking chairs.
John's wife had passed away two years earlier, and I could
tell he was lonely. He fussed over Winston and said the
dog was welcome to stay in for the night if I liked.

John no longer had a dog, and he never did let them
in the house, but I could see he missed having one
around. He knocked tobacco out of his pipe and into the
top opening of the stove and then refilled it. Striking a
wooden match on the side of the hot stove, he sucked
the pipe to life.

John knows more about prairie grouse than most
folks. He is one of the few ranchers I've known who
doesn't accuse predators of evil acts. In fact, he and his
son won't let anyone kill coyotes or foxes on their ranch.
John calls them "gopher exterminators."

He's also a self-taught biologist and well read on the
ecology of prairie grouse. He wanted to talk about grouse
then and knew I was always ready to listen.

"Today's conditions have made the birds change their
habits to some extent." John explained. "Prairie chickens
are more predictable than sharptails in their daily and sea-

sonal movements, but reading the bird's habitat and learning their daily movements is the key to finding their locations. The prairie is usually the best bet to find chickens. I look for uncut croplands adjacent to or within large grasslands. Grouse feed in these places in the morning and then return to their prairie hangouts close by.

"Chickens fly to and from their feeding areas morning and evening. But the exact time of day depends on the weather. If it's clear after feeding for a couple of hours the prairie chickens hit the grassland slopes below the higher ridges, then loaf, sun, and preen themselves.

"Prairie chickens prefer these places for several reasons: they can look out across the prairie for danger; the sidehills become warm from the sun; and the bunch grasses on the slopes are good areas to chase insects. These open areas also provide good dusting places. Chickens do not like to get wet, and the sunny slopes are the first places the morning dew dries."

We'd talked about all of this many times, but I let him go on because I enjoy hearing him talk about something we both love.

After the short biology lesson, I suggested we get some sleep.

We took our time going to the old home place, driving the country roads and looking for flying prairie chickens coming off their feeding areas. We didn't see any birds, so we assumed they had already moved. The sun was high when we turned into the farmhouse lane. John checked the mailbox and came back empty-handed.

Getting back in the pickup, he said, "They must

have picked up the mail last evening. The sidehills are warming up. I'll bet the birds are taking their sun baths below the ridges."

I drove a mile down the lane, crossed the cattle guard, and entered the cut hayfield. I parked the pickup next to a grassy draw that snakes its way through the hay meadow. A light breeze stirred the golden seed heads in the grassy draw.

I let three Britts out of the dog compartments and put beeper collars on them while John slid our shotguns out of their leather cases. When it comes to prairie grouse hunting, I prefer a light 20-gauge. John's gun is a light 12-gauge side-by-side. He doesn't like the smaller bores, but knows I do. He also knows that I'm more interested in Winston getting into birds than shooting. One or two chickens is enough for me.

John's plan was to skirt the cut hayfield first and see if any birds are still feeding. Based on years of experience, John's theory is that young birds sometimes linger in the open fields longer than mature birds. But he doesn't know why. I have my doubts, but it's worth working the edges anyway, and I don't question his reasoning.

The Brittanys had a different idea. With their beepers sounding, they disappeared into the tall grass of a nearby draw in search of pheasants. Several big roosters came boiling out of the grass two hundred yards ahead before I could get the dogs turned in our direction. I said a few words under my breath.

John was laughing. "The dogs are having a little fun, Ben."

This was Winston's first encounter with pheasants, and they were driving him nuts. I bore down on the whistle again and he reluctantly returned.

Thirty minutes passed, and other than the pheasants the dogs never seemed birdy. Knowing that prairie chickens like to stay put at midday, we walked toward the low hills. The sun had warmed the prairie, and the dogs checked in and got a little water. We rested several minutes before starting up the gradual slope toward a high ridge.

Three-quarters of the way up the dogs disappeared over the other side of the ridge. Before we reached the top, the beepers were sounding the hawk scream, telling me the dogs were pointing. I headed toward the sound just as two prairie chickens sailed overhead, too high to shoot. They coasted down the slope, crossed the hay meadow, and disappeared into the distant hills on the other side of the field.

On top of the ridge and short of breath, John and I hurried down the slope to the three dogs, who had remained motionless. They were lined up perfectly, like they were laid out with a string. John and I walked slowly past Mac, then Shoe. Winston was ten steps ahead.

Not saying a word, I motioned to John to keep moving just as five chickens feathered the light breeze and turned downwind, flying over our heads and following the same flight path as the first two birds. The last three dove over the crest of the hill and were gone. We shot and feathers drifted slowly down as Shoe and Mac retrieved the brace of barred chickens to me.

Winston had missed the retrieving action by following the birds over the hill, but he came back to look for the downed birds. I didn't say a word to him because I was sure he just keyed in on the wrong bird. I had seen this happen many times when a covey or flock of birds flushed. Dogs are no different than we are. We all need to concentrate on one single bird.

After two days of hard hunting, all five Brittanys had had a serious workout. It was time for a day's rest as we moved on to Valentine, Nebraska.

To the south, the horizon was dark and unfriendly. Rain cut into the dust, making streaks across the windshield. Water, mud, and road grime slapped the side of the pickup with each passing vehicle.

The odometer read 950 miles. For the past forty miles I had been driving through a landscape filled with miles of lush, wet grass, sculptured sand hills, and small creeks. I turned off the highway and onto a narrow lane, the tires squeezing water out of the sandy soil as we made tracks on the road.

My friend Ray was already there. I packed my gear into a lovely old farmhouse built not long after the homesteaders arrived. It's a modest affair, with a few old collectable treasures in every room, each with its own story. It reminds me of the farmhouse I lived in as a boy.

Looking over the yard, I could see rain settle softly on the Sand Hills. I fed and exercised the dogs at dusk before turning in to the sound of distant rumblings from storm clouds all around us. Heavy raindrops splattered on the metal roof as I crawled into bed.

Another successful retrieve and delivery.

The wet weather did not move out overnight. Water dripped from everything, and the forecast was for more rain. I was watching what looked like a gallon of coffee perk on the wood stove. Ray was fixing a huge breakfast, and Shoe and Mac were curled up under the kitchen table. Winston was begging Ray for food. Five dogs in the kitchen is a bit much, so the other two were in their kennel boxes. They would have their turn.

The drive over several miles of soaked, sandy roads and through the super-saturated wet hills had a sobering effect on us. Winston was in the backseat of the extended cab looking out the window. He was wet but in high spirits. After riding for some time, we spotted a small flock of chickens on a sparsely-covered hill. They glided off as the hunting rig approached. Winston saw them too, pressing his nose against the glass and fogging up the window.

In shifts, all the dogs got to work the wet cover. The morning came and went and no birds were found. To save time, we ate lunch while driving to a new location. It was the only dry place we could find anyway.

I explained John's prairie chicken theory to Ray. "The wet weather is the main factor in not finding birds. Scenting conditions are extremely poor for the dogs. The rain washes scent away, and the wet vegetation forces birds into extremely sparse cover. In open cover, prairie grouse use their eyes and wing off long before a hunter sees them."

Ray nodded in agreement.

The next stop was at the edge of miles and miles of

vast open rolling hills and sand dunes. Ray and I walked the tough, sandy terrain with three dogs working far ahead of us. But none of us complained. The rain added a softness to the light and led me to wonder why the landscape had changed so abruptly. The Sand Hills can be intimidating when you are walking long distances.

Like morning, afternoon passed quietly, and then early evening was upon us. I put all five dogs down, but still no birds. We were soaked. Like foot soldiers, we walked miles in the wet hills.

The dogs did make two finds. On the first, all five Brittanys locked up tight on a single adult male prairie chicken that flushed far out of shooting range. On the second, we found Winston pointing a box turtle. He brought it back to me, proud of his find. I thanked him. All the dogs were wet and tired from working hard all day, so we headed for the pickup.

Back at the farmhouse, Ray and I prepared supper as the dogs slept in a pile under the kitchen table.

We had spent the day in country that's a secluded prairie chicken heaven, although sometimes we mere mortals have no influence on the weather or the chickens. But being able to walk through such a beautiful landscape offset the loss of a handful of feathers. Chickens or no chickens, I wouldn't trade the last two days of hunting with Ray.

At daybreak, Ray left for Oklahoma. I hit the road as well, and as I watched the weather slowly clear, my thoughts turned to old friends and the hunting still ahead.

The Rolm ranch in South Dakota is close to the
Montana border and five hundred miles from Valentine,
Nebraska. It's a long drive, and I continued to travel the
blue highways instead of the gravel roads. I had prom-
ised Marvin that we'd hunt birds a couple of days with
Winston. Marvin loves Winston as much as I do, but he
doesn't let on. Maybe he doesn't want the other Brittanys
to think he plays favorites.

I first met Marvin when he was still cutting his baby
teeth, but this year he turned twenty-one. Several years
ago Marvin had a serious accident while working cattle
on a motorbike. The bike flipped over and landed on his
head. The medical complications left him paralyzed on
the dominant side of his body. After two years of physi-
cal therapy, counseling, and much determination on his
part, Marvin's speech and walking ability greatly
improved. At this time, the fingers of his right hand are
not one hundred percent, but knowing Marvin, I'll bet
they will be in the future. In the meantime, he's done
remarkably well using his left hand. "The only difference
in using the other hand," he says, "is that it takes a little
longer to get the chores done."

Marvin does around ninety percent of the farming
on the family's large cattle ranch. To put the amount of
labor he does in perspective, just stacking the huge
round hay bails from the cut fields takes over three
weeks, working twelve to fourteen hours a day.

Marvin and I started hunting birds together back
when he could hardly carry a shotgun. Even then he
was a natural shot. But after the accident, he had to

start shooting left-handed. He carries a 28-gauge side-by-side shotgun and can bring the gun up with one arm, slide the safety off, and shoot extremely fast. Some guys are at their best in difficult circumstances. Marvin's just that way.

Over the next two days, with the help of Winston and the other dogs, Marvin collected enough Huns and sharptails for several fine wild gamebird meals for the whole family.

Another morning came and it was time to pull stakes and head out. There wasn't a cloud in the sky, not a breath of wind. The dogs had had two great days of hunting and Marvin had shot well. Before I even left the yard, Marvin had his tractor up and running.

Driving home, I thought about the new places I'd been, the friends I'd seen both new and old, the dog work from Winston and the rest of the Brittanys, and the pleasure of driving uncrowded country roads.

To me, gravel roads, gun dogs, and good folks just go together.

Shooting the High Plains

Nick North and I were hunting gray partridge on my home turf when the subject of another partridge came up.

"If you want Winston to get into high plains chukars," Nick said casually, "I think it can be arranged."

That evening after dinner he pointed to a spot on a map. "Ben," he said, "I have a friend who owns six miles of Meadow Creek. I hunted the place years ago, and it's always good. The country's been dry for several years so the birds may be concentrated in lower elevations along the creek where there is more water. When I get back, I'll give him a call and see how the chukar population is doing. If that doesn't pan out, there's public land farther south we can go to."

Within a week, Nick called to say that the rancher at Meadow Creek had seen birds all summer, but didn't know what the population looked like now. "Ben, my friend said he has a double-wide we can stay in. By the way, he said there's quail too."

"Valley quail, I presume."

"Yep, there are lots of them along the creek."

So at sunrise, I was behind the wheel of the K-9

Hilton, headed for chukar country. I made two stops to exercise the dogs and three others for coffee and gas. The sun was low when I finally turned off the paved road. The next seventeen miles were all sand and dust.

Lengthening shadows danced along the sun-baked, sagebrush hills. Farther on, the hills gave way to steep rugged canyons, their narrow knife-edged ridges standing like castles in the fading sunlight. A dust devil twisted in front of the hunting rig, following the sandy road a short way before disappearing into the purple sage. I looked at Winston, who was sitting in the front seat, and said, "Chukars live in this moonscape."

Nick was right, the country needed rain. Every time I slowed down to look at a different large red-rock formation, a cloud of dust caught up with the rig and blocked the view. I was hoping that the wind would bring some much-needed moisture, but it was probably just another dry front passing through the arid west.

Finally, I crossed the last of many cattle guards and parked next to the double-wide. The sun had set behind a distant wall of rock, but I still had time to exercise the dogs in the last of the light.

I ran the six Brittanys for fifteen minutes, then fed and kenneled five of them for the night. Winston I took in the house with me.

He barged through the door, greeted Nicks, then knocked over Rose, Nick's old English setter, who met him with a growl. "Winston leave her alone," I yelled.

Nick had been putting groceries in the refrigerator, and he stopped to shake my hand. Over supper and a cold beer, we talked weather, dogs, birds, and places to hunt the next day.

Morning came early. The smell of fresh coffee filled the air.

We both took our pickup trucks so his dog Rose could rest in her own kennel box when I was running my dogs. Rose didn't like all the male dogs anyway, and I can't say I blamed her. They just wouldn't leave the old girl alone.

We crossed Meadow Creek, which meanders through the narrow valley where the original homestead once was. It was the only flat acreage within miles. Cottonwoods, willows, cattails, and mixed riparian grasses and forbs lined the creek. During the summer a manmade ditch feeds precious water to the hay meadow then overflows into a swampy arm of the creek. But today it was bone dry.

A big bunch of valley quail ran down the dirt lane in front of us, then flew back toward the heavy cover along the creek. Both Nick and I stopped and watched the birds, but this morning we were after chukars.

A ranch hand suggested earlier that we hunt around a stock tank in the hills. While working cattle, he had seen a lot of chukars in that area. Nick put his setters to work on the slope above the dry water tank. I hunted Winston and Pat below the tank, where water once seeped down.

We hunted for a couple of hours, and I put fresh dogs down often. It seemed like the dogs had covered every square foot of the rugged country within a mile of the stock tank. Several times they pointed, but turned up nothing. I did find some old droppings and dusting holes. Either the country was so dry that the chukars had moved to a lower elevation in search of greens to eat, or the scenting conditions were so poor that the dogs had simply missed the birds.

In the afternoon, we hunted an irrigation ditch that ran along a large hayfield. Puddles of stagnant water dotted the bottom of the ditch, and both of the dogs we had down ran through the muddy holes, drinking as they went.

"That water ought to make the dogs sick," I called to Nick.

On the other side of the ditch was a steep sagebrush slope with a ribbon of red rhyolite formations outlined against the distant horizon. It wasn't long before Nick's setter Rose locked up, her tail high.

Winston was running through the hayfield and didn't see Rose stop. A chukar flushed and Nick put it on the ground, then the big covey split. Most went toward the top of the ridge, while others appeared to follow the ditch around the hill.

Winston heard the shot and came back. He watched Rose make the retrieve to Nick.

I climbed the sagebrush slope with Winston out in front while Nick followed the other birds around the ditch. I slowly worked diagonally up the talus slope, climbed a huge rock outcropping, then stopped to catch my breath just below the rhyolite formations. Two shots rang out from below.

I had forgotten to put a beeper collar on Winston, so

once on top I scanned the deep canyon below for movement. Winston was nowhere to be seen, and I could only assume he's pointing.

From this vantage point a hogback leading down to the bottom of the canyon was the only place not in view. I figured there was a depression beyond the hogback. That was the only place Winston could be. I hurried down the steep rocky slope, sliding as I went.

I worked my way up the other side of the rugged incline and looked into a grassy depression. Winston was standing rock solid, the sun illuminating his white coat. Before I could get to him the dry, golden cheatgrass seemed to come alive. Five chukars burst skyward and then dove down the steep slope. Slipping, I got off a lucky shot with my 20-gauge side-by-side. A single chukar fell, coming to rest at the bottom of the incline. The blast echoed over and over along the rocky canyon walls. Then silence returned.

I lost sight of Winston as he went down the rocky slope after the bird. I was hoping he could figure out how to return the same way he went down. Minutes passed, and not quite believing my eyes, I saw a small white speck working its way toward me. "Come on, Winston," I shouted, and it echoed off the canyon walls: *Come onnnnn Winstonnnnnn Winstonnnnnnnn.*

"Good dog, good dog," I kept yelling. It seemed like forever before he fought his way back to me. Winston dropped the bird at my feet, then lay down, panting and licking a bloody front paw. I sat beside him, giving him a pat and examining his pad.

A small, sharp rock was imbedded in his paw. I dug it out with my pocketknife. Winston fought it, but he knew I was helping him. A small flesh wound was exposed on his pad. I let him up and he was off again, not even limping. "You're one tough dog," I called to him, but he was already out of earshot.

I met Nick back at the pickups, and we called it quits for the day. Nick had four chukars; I collected one. Not bad for a chukar hunt. Late afternoon, Nick and I worked the other dogs on a covey of valley quail. Winston's paw looked a bit sore, so I put him up for the day. He cried a sad song as we headed off without him.

The next morning Nick and I decided to split up to cover more country and maybe locate where the birds are concentrating. Some time later I was looking to the horizon above the ridge. The steep canyon was a rugged landscape of bluffs, talus and sagebrush slopes, rocky outcroppings, and barren windswept ridges. I saw Winston pointing high on the crest of the ridge, and thought to myself that chukars are tough birds, and hunting them is for the young, or at least the young at heart.

When I finally reached the top of the ridge, my heart was beating fast, my legs ached, and the chukars were gone. Winston was far below, again on point and waiting for me to catch up. Sliding slowly down the talus slope I tried not to start a mini avalanche, as the birds flushed again out of gun range. Seven or eight birds glided off and landed in a large patch of cheatgrass on the opposite side of the canyon. Looking straight across at them, the chukars seemed the size of mosquitoes.

Winston stood motionless for a moment watching the birds land. Then down he went and up the other side, pointing the birds above him. After taking a deep breath, I hoofed it to the bottom of the dry wash and up again toward the birds. I puffed up the steep incline and moved beyond Winston, anticipating a flush. But no chukars. I stopped, looked back at the dog, and called, "Winston!" Then, one by one, they came up.

Two partridge tumbled. Winston picked up the first bird as it rolled down the rocky incline, then tried to retrieve the second with the other bird still in his mouth. I reloaded and knocked down a straggler. Winston looked a bit confused as he tried to figure out how to retrieve three downed birds at once.

I had lucked out—most times chukars aren't this easy!

I met up with Nick and learned that he had found a large bunch of birds several coulees over from where I'd been hunting. We put Winston and Rose up for the day and worked the other dogs.

Nick killed five birds by early afternoon. I shot one more, and we called it quits for the day.

On the third morning, Nick and I went to the same area. Nick continued walking the main canyon, but I heard water running in a narrow draw so I motioned to Nick that I was splitting off.

Winston also heard the live spring and ran toward the sound. Halfway over, he slammed to a stop just as a huge covey of valley quail exploded, scattering and landing above the spring. Within minutes Winston stood motionless again. After I shot, he retrieved his first valley quail.

Critics, past and present, have given the valley quail a bum rap. They say the birds congregate in large flocks and can't be approached within shotgun range or that they're notorious runners who rarely fly or that coveys can't be broken up and can't be worked with pointing dogs or even that valley quail are too small a target and not worth shooting.

I would have to agree that valley quail form large flocks, can be notorious runners, and make small targets. But I disagree that working them with pointing dogs is impossible or that they aren't worth the trouble.

Looking left, I saw my hunting partner working his way toward the other dogs who were on point in heavy cover. There was no reason to quicken my pace. Nick pushed hard through a dry, chest-high tangle of tumble-weed, held for years in the brambles. The large curled blackberry leaves clung fragilely to the vines, falling as Nick passed. He moved toward the sounds of the dogs' beepers. The high-pitched hawk screams indicated that two dogs were on point.

The sounds were coming from the center of a large briar patch beneath the high cover. The dogs were not visible. Holding his gun high, Nick was doing the best he could. Even seeing the quail flush was doubtful, but someone had to get to the dogs on point.

On my left, a long narrow row of prairie cotton-woods stood tall along the wide irrigation ditch. Both sides of the ditch had trees. High pigweed, stripped of

Winston retrieving a valley quail (above). The high plains are rugged and beautiful country.

foliage, had dropped its shining circular seeds on the ground. Good food for valley quail, I thought, and this was an ideal place to find them.

I looked around and it seemed the only departure route for the birds was through the line of trees. But even if the quail flew out on my side, getting a shot would be questionable.

There was a roar of wings and a large covey of valley quail flushed, but no shots were fired. The quail simply flew low toward the trees, made a sharp turn to the left, followed the ditch for thirty yards, crossed the creek, and continued up the hill, fanning out on a small at bench full of bunchgrass and mixed sagebrush.

There was a steep rocky ridge two hundred yards above the spot where the birds had come down. I was sure we couldn't walk above them, but they also couldn't go over the top without flying.

I watched the hillside for any movement as Nick crashed through the heavy brush, crossing over to my side of the ditch. By the time we lay out a strategy for how to approach the scattered birds, the dogs were already on point thirty yards below where the main bunch landed, held by scent carried down on a soft breeze.

The four dogs looked like white stones, motionless against a backdrop of waving gold bunchgrass and purple-green sage. We both pushed up the hill, slowly passed Winston, and then stopped.

"The dogs sure have 'em pinned down," I said, looking over at Nick. And therein lies one of the secrets of

hunting valley quail: After the first flush, the quail usually hold tight for pointing dogs.

It was a beautiful sight; a picture of Winston I won't
soon forget.

They Got 'Em

Years ago I lived near the Okanogan Valley not far from Wenatchee, Washington. It's a beautiful area, with high lakes, fast-falling streams, and a diversity of flora and fauna in the surrounding mountains. Although I hunted eight different game bird species there, mountain quail were the toughest—with or without dogs.

My introduction to hunting mountain quail came through a wildlife biologist friend named Brad. We had many interests in common and kicked around together fly-fishing high mountain lakes and hunting game birds in rugged terrain.

When I eventually moved on to Montana, Brad and I continued to correspond with one another and fished Yellowstone National Park a time or two. But that was about it. We talked about hunting birds again, but his preference was still the mountains of Washington and my focus was hunting in Montana.

That was until Winston came into my life. As a young dog, he excelled so much at pointing and retrieving different species of game bird that it led me to alter my hunting plans. I really wanted to give

Winston the opportunity to hunt every upland game bird in North America.

So I gave my old friend a call. I wanted to take Winston back to some of the same areas I hunted many years before for chukar and mountain quail.

Like me, Brad had retired from a lifelong occupation, but he still worked as a wildlife habitat consultant. And he was still knowledgeable on the whereabouts of game birds and tuned in to the best areas to hunt each year.

I suggested we meet in eastern Washington, but he informed me that the mountain quail population had declined where we had hunted together years before. If I wanted to get into good numbers, he said, I would have to come farther west to where he lived. Brad also mentioned that he was in between bird dogs. I was sorry to hear he had lost his old English setter, but if I knew Brad, he wouldn't be without a bird dog for long.

"Are you going to get another setter?" I asked.

"You know, Ben, I'm researching several other pointing breeds to replace her. I'm even thinking maybe a Brittany."

"Don't jump to any outrageous conclusions, Brad," I said, laughing.

"I've always liked your Britts, even though I like a long-tailed dog when hunting in the woods."

"Well, if you get a Britt just don't get her tail cut off. The dog won't know the difference."

"No, but I would," he laughed.

Brad was delighted when I told him about my new young dog Winston.

"I can't wait to see Winston," he said, "and from what you've said he sounds like a dandy. Are you going to bring some other dogs?"

"Oh, yes, but I'm not sure which ones, other than Winston and Shoe."

After our phone conversation the plan was set. I'd drive straight to Brad's home and stay with him. He had told me he had access to good mountain quail hunting on private land in the foothills of the coastal Cascade Range. And he emphasized that he had seen good numbers of young birds while doing habitat reconstruction.

It sounded like an ideal place to introduce Winston to mountain quail. After chasing mountain quail, my plan was to hunt eastern Washington for chukar and valley quail. Winston had already added these two birds to his list, but I would never pass up a chance to hunt them.

Brad had said that if he could break away he'd come along for a couple of days. And for Brad to leave his beloved mountains during grouse season was a true sacrifice. As he didn't have a dog, I think the idea of seeing a young Brittany at work intrigued him, especially as it was one of the breeds he was interested in.

So I packed up all my gear and followed the interstate through Spokane, Washington, stopping for the night at a motel in Moses Lake.

When I took a break to gas up, an old farmer in bib overalls walked over and asked to see my bird dogs.

"I used to hunt pheasants with my dog when I was young," he said. "My question to you, young man, is why would you leave Montana to hunt in Washington?"

I showed him Winston and explained that my goal was to get my young bird dog on as many different upland birds as possible. "There are certain game birds you have here that we don't in Montana," I said. "And I want to give Winston the chance to point and retrieve every game bird in North America."

Then the old man went on, complaining, "We had plenty of pheasants when I was a boy, but today they're gone where I used to live and farm. I'm an old wind-break, but small farms save the earth, and the big corporate farms kill the earth."

"I couldn't agree more. I'll keep that in mind when looking for places to hunt," I said.

The two-lane blacktop road I was traveling the next morning divided miles and miles of rolling wheatfields that were harvested weeks before. It was yellow from horizon to horizon, with only this black strip of road to break up the pattern. I wondered if the old gentleman I met used to farm somewhere nearby.

I arrived at Brad's home just as the western hills blocked the last rays of sunlight. We got our plans set for the morning's hunt, then spent some time catching up.

The hill dropped down to Pass Creek Road, then went up the other side. We turned off the gravel, and stopped at a locked metal gate. I unlocked it and swung it open, and Brad's pickup jumped past me. I closed the gate and hopped back in the truck. We rattled our way up the washboard hill, with the dog boxes shifting back a bit on the steep incline. The pickup kicked gravel from the two-track until it topped out and started down the other side. This was repeated for several more hills before we came to a stop.

"On a warm morning like this, they'd be somewhere along the creek or in the vicinity of the springs. If we're going to find them, they are going to be close by," Brad explains. "I saw twelve birds last week, but I never got a shot at them."

"In one covey?"

"Yeah," Brad answers.

"That's a big covey for mountain quail."

"You bet it is. This is the best year I've seen in a long time. That not only goes for the number of birds in a covey, but also the number of coveys I've found. The spring hatch was good and the young birds had lots of insects to feed on. This year there is good cover and water everywhere. And we may find them anywhere.

"I've done a lot of work to rehabilitate the birds' cover, and it sure has paid off. For the past few years this has been my favorite place to hunt mountain quail."

"If I recall, it's almost like the forest you and I hunted years ago in eastern Washington. These mixed forests with rolling hills and woody draws are beautiful. And the high Cascades in the background make this a picturesque place."

"Over there," he said, pointing his finger, "the next draw is another place I'll take you if we have time. As the crow flies, it's not far from here. It's a burned-over area. And mountain quail particularly like areas that have been timbered off or burned. This year there is abundant re-growth, which provides both food and cover—and water.

"Mountain quail are early risers and feed at first light. So by now they should be done feeding and on their way to water. Midday, they loaf and dust under thick overhead cover close to a spring or stream. That's where I spotted them last week, but the cover was too heavy to get a shot. Hopefully they'll still be traveling to water so the dogs can find them on the move. That sure helps the dogs to scent them. By late afternoon the birds are on the move again and return to forage until dusk, then drink once more before going to roost.

"Let's start by searching the edges around heavy cover, Ben, and then listen for birds calling and look for tracks."

"This cover looks quite thick, so I think I'm going to put just two dogs down to start with and see how it goes," I responded.

I handed Brad a bell and he put it on Mac while I wrestled one onto Winston, who pulled away then ran off straight down the dirt road. Mac started to work the heavy cover to my left.

I whistled Winston back. He came reluctantly, and I told him to hunt the cover. He looked at me like I was nuts. "Get in there, Winston, you little varmint!"

Brad laughed as Winston ran down the logging trail. After a short time, he broke into the heavy cover and was gone. The only sounds we heard were the two bells, telling us where the dogs were.

We walked an old road that Brad had seeded to grass in order to stop erosion, and he mentioned that the road led to a spring. Brad watched the edges of the cover and his side of the road; I watched the other side. The two Britts showed little interest and came back periodically to check in.

It was a bright day, still and cloudless. Scenting conditions should have been fine with all the moisture around, and there was plenty of water for the dogs to drink. But sometimes conditions can appear fine, yet not pan out like they should.

We spent a good part of the day walking the areas where Brad saw birds the week before. We went to the burned-over forests and followed an old logging trail not traveled for years. There was evidence that the birds had been around, but both the tracks and droppings were old. We never heard or saw a quail.

By late afternoon, we were hungry and tired and the two braces of dogs we'd used seemed played out, so we called it quits.

Driving back to his house, I said, "Well, Brad, that's mountain quail hunting like I remember it."

"The birds are there and it's big country with heavy cover," Brad responded. "The dogs just have to run into them. Let's start early tomorrow and see if we can find them feeding in more open country."

The next morning Winston woke me to let him out. I was up before the sun rose above the horizon. Brad poured me a cup of coffee and packed lunch, while I fed the dogs. We ate sweet rolls and drank coffee on the drive out.

The sun still hadn't come over the hills when I again swung open the metal gate. Brad drove through with the headlights off. We stopped at the same place as the day before and opened the windows to just listen for a while.

I was sipping coffee when Brad said softly, "Did you hear that?"

"No, I didn't."

"It's a male mountain quail. But it sounds a long way off. The sound is coming from the opposite direction we hunted yesterday. I think I know about where they are.

"Ben, listen, it's a sharp whistle."

Kow, kow, kow, kow, kow interrupted the silent forest.

"I hear it."

Brad put his finger to his mouth, signaling me to talk softly.

"It's the assembly call. The birds must be scattered or possibly moving to feed."

I nodded, thinking that if the birds are scattered they won't run as much. I planned on taking my old dog Shoe along with Winston this morning, hoping Winston would get his first point on mountain quail.

"Brad," I said in a low voice, holding up two fingers, "I'm just going to take two dogs."

"That's okay with me," he whispered back.

Quietly, we slipped on vests and ready the guns. I put the dogs on the ground without bells or beepers. We walked carefully along an overgrown logging road, moving toward the calling bird in the distance.

Shoe heard the bird calling and slowed to a walk. Winston kept moving far ahead as a single bird flushed off to our left. I whistled Winston back, and three more quail flushed from a small patch of cover surrounded by grass.

"I don't think that's Winston fault," I explained to Brad. "Neither dog seemed to smell birds. They were far off the dogs' scent line. Shoe slowed down because he associated the sound he heard with game birds. I'm sure Winston hasn't recognized that sound yet, but I'll bet he will next time."

We turned left and after a hundred yards or so reached a hilltop, following the direction we thought the quail flew. The forest became clear of understory as we walked down a rocky trail.

"Brad," I asked, "when was the last time you saw the dogs?"

"Just before we broke over the top of the hill. I think they turned and are hunting below the ridge."

"I thought they went over the top, but I'll bet you're right. This side doesn't look like mountain quail cover. It's too open. I think the dogs are in back of us and off to the side, like you said."

"Should we split up, Ben?"

"I don't think so. Let's both go back and look for the dogs. They could be pointing. I don't have any sound devices on them, and the cover back there is heavy. We'll just have to try to spot them if they're still on point."

We crossed back over the hill and stayed below the meandering ridge, both looking down into the brushy draw. The heat had long cut the morning dew, and sweat rolled down the back of my neck.

It seemed like the dogs had been gone for over twenty minutes. I thought about blowing the whistle, but if they were pointing they wouldn't come anyway—unless

I blew my head off fifty times. So I remained silent, searching the heavy cover as I walked.

"Ben," Brad called softly, "come here."

He pointed downhill and I walked over and followed the sightline of his finger. Finally, I saw it: a white spot under some heavily-tangled berry bushes.

"I think that's Shoe. Let's go!"

Halfway down, where the buckbrush joins the rose brambles, I spotted Winston. I turned and looked at Brad, pointing downhill, and he nodded his head.

Farther down, along an old irrigation ditch that ran along the base of the hill I clearly saw both dogs. Winston moved slowly out in front of Shoe, then stopped.

"Darn him," I said softly to myself.

Brad moved off to my right, and I motioned him to keep going. I walked past Shoe and stopped alongside Winston. Brad was twenty yards to the right and a little ahead of me. I signaled to him that I was going in just as the brush exploded. Birds seemed to be going in every direction.

I missed an easy shot. Shifting left, I fired and missed again. Most of the birds flushed up the hill to my left. I never heard Brad shoot and figured no birds flew his way, but then Winston brought me a beautiful mountain quail.

"Brad," I yelled, "Winston retrieved your quail to me, but I didn't even hear you shoot."

Walking over, he asked, "How did you do?"

"I missed both birds. Thank goodness you got one

As always, Winston was eager to start hunting, this time for mountain quail.

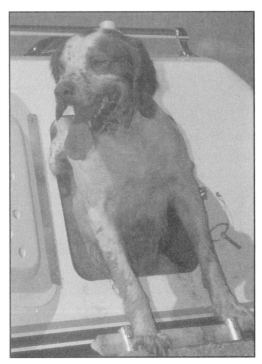

for Winston. I was thinking it was a single from the covey that we flushed earlier. And when the whole covey exploded I got frustrated and blew it. That's the best excuse I can think of."

Brad grinned and so do I.

The past two days had been a blast, and it was after nine by the time I left. Winston didn't outperform his dad, Shoe, but he came close.

The score went like this: eight finds for Shoe, six for Winston, six for Mac, and three for Pat. Our bag limits did not equal what the dogs found, of course, but that's mountain quail hunting. Not bad for two guys and four dogs.

As I drove off, I was already picturing the chukar and valley quail hunting awaiting us over the eastern horizon.

The Same Fine Bird

In many ways, the Midwestern bobwhite quail differs from its cousin in the East, but it's still the same fine game bird. It can often be found where cropland and open prairie merge with riparian forests along waterways and brushy draws. Hedges and windbreaks of Osage orange, Russian olive, caragana, and green ash are also some of the quail's favorite hiding places, and they're often close to where farmers store their grain. It's easy to underestimate the speed of quail heading for the nearest cover in open country. They can disappear before a shot is fired.

One of the best ways to hunt these open-country bobwhites is with big-running pointing dogs like Winston.

I was having breakfast with a rancher in a small cafe in Nebraska. In front of me was a cup of black, black coffee, ranch-cured bacon, farm-fresh eggs, and homemade toast. I first met this man and his wife when they were fishing in Montana, and they invited me to hunt quail on their land.

After breakfast, we headed out to check on the quail.

The first point came in the center of a weedy caragana and Osage orange shelterbelt. The three Brittanys were lined up in a row, with heads cocked slightly downward. They appeared to be pointing the Osage orange balls lying on the black dirt. Other than the green balls, the ground was as clean and at as a pool table. Confident that there were no quail, I stepped in front of Winston and kicked a large green ball. I practically stepped on the covey of quail, which immediately exploded in my face. I panicked and missed.

The dogs crashed through the shelterbelt and out the other side. I was feeling depressed as I heard my hunting partner shoot. He called the dogs to hunt dead, and Winston brought me a male bobwhite. By late afternoon we scattered six coveys. I did better on singles, shooting five birds over Winston.

After Nebraska I continued on to Kansas to meet an old friend I hadn't seen in years. Art and I were hunting bobwhites not far from the Flint Hills when Winston made game, pointing into a marshy area. A woodcock uttered, then flushed, but neither of us shot. I wasn't sure if the state had a season for this pretty little game bird.

My hunting partner said with slight disgust, "I don't shoot swamp chickens."

"Is there a season here?" I asked.

"Oh, yes, but they're not worth eating."

"I disagree, Art. And Winston just pointed that bird. I've never shot a woodcock over him."

"Let me tell you about woodcock hunters, Ben. I'm

talking about these addicts east of the Mississippi. These guys claim that woodcock hunting is an upland-shooting tradition for northerners on par with that found on southern plantations for the gentleman bobwhite. They spend more time trying to get the right gun than any other upland bird hunter I can think of.

"Some also believe that woodcock are the toughest targets to shoot. And for some reason this game bird is valued highly as a delicacy. Oh, yes, the bird is hung and the entrails never removed, and then it's cooked rare. Ben, for god's sake, these birds eat worms!"

I laughed as his diatribe winded down and said, "Well, this is still a good chance for Winston to get a woodcock."

"I'll take my dog and hunt along the fence next to that CRP field while you look for that swamp chicken," he replied. "By the way, the bobwhites we flushed went that way, too. You may find them. If I don't see you in an hour, meet me back at the truck. Don't linger too long chasing that crazy bird. Early afternoon, my plan is to hunt the Flint Hills."

Still chuckling at Art's powerful opinion about woodcock, I called Winston over and headed for the lowlands.

I started working through a grassy slough. It was too wet to plow and surrounded by sumac, which still had a little dried fruit hanging on. Beyond the sumacs the floor of the oak forest lifted gradually under a blanket of decomposed autumn leaves.

It was a picture-perfect location for woodcock. I

assumed the bird we flushed went down close to the sumacs and the forest edge at the far end of the slough. Winston made several casts in the open grassy area without success. He swung toward a clump of sumacs and slowed before freezing into a point. A single bobwhite flushed twenty yards ahead and flew toward the hardwoods. Before I reached the end of the slough another quail buzzed out ahead of Winston and took the same route.

I was wondering why the quail were so spooky. It occurred to me that the last bobwhite had flushed from about the same spot where I marked the woodcock. But Winston covered the area well and never made game. He didn't show any interest whatsoever, so I looped back by way of the woods, hoping to run into the quail.

Fifty yards into the hardwood forest, I was walking between two large oaks when Winston topped the small rise we were on and slammed into a point. His body was twisted sideways and his head appeared to be buried in a patch of high grass. I heard his beeper collar sound the point mode.

In my mind I was seeing woodcock, but in this kind of grass it had to be a bobwhite quail. I walked up to Winston and tried to read his thoughts, searching for an image of the bird before us. Turning to the cover, I visualized a large dark-brown object with a long beak and big eyes holding at against the ground.

I kicked the cover once, twice, then again. I was still thinking big woodcock for some reason when a small, fast object flushed underfoot. The shot echoed through

A bobwhite quail (above), and the old farmstead we hunted them on (below).

the woods, and a bobwhite hen zipped around a tree. Disgusted, I didn't take a second shot.

Winston pointed again within a hundred yards. This time I moved past him confidently. After the flush, a clear shot sounded and feathers drifted down on the breeze, settling on the dry leaves below. This time I was thinking bobwhite, and I centered the bird.

Art was eating lunch when I got back to the truck.

"Heard you shoot twice, Ben. Did Winston find that swamp chicken for you?"

"No, he didn't. He made two solid points, both on single bobwhites. I missed the first bird, but got the second. He also made a nice retrieve."

Another year would pass before Winston pointed and retrieved his first beautiful woodcock. I hung this fine little bird for a couple of days and then cooked it very rare—but without the entrails. And I said to myself that even though it does eat worms, woodcock are indeed a delicacy.

No matter where you hunt woodcock or bobwhites, they are still the same fine bird.

Tracks

When the leaves turn color in the fall, hunters in large numbers take to the field to pursue North America's most popular upland game bird, the pheasant. For many hunters, there's nothing more exciting than the sight of a cackling rooster taking flight and nothing so fine as a proud dog retrieving a beautiful bouquet of feathers.

This may come as a surprise to some folks, but even though I've had pointing dogs for most of my life, I'm not convinced they are the best dog for hunting wild pheasants. I believe that flushing dogs and retrievers are better suited for chasing these birds. My dogs are big-running animals that get out and move. And wide-ranging dogs and wild, running pheasants just don't mix.

Personally, I'd just as soon not hunt pheasants. It's not in my dogs' best interest. A hunter who works his pointing dog on wild pheasants and then hunts other game birds is going to see his canine friend make mistakes. This isn't the dog's fault; it's just that he's still focused on those "crazy pheasants."

So while I could have added pheasants to the four other game birds Winston pointed and retrieved during his first year, I chose not to. I just didn't want him to work these speedy runners too early in his career.

Winston surprised me when the time finally came, though, for it didn't take long for him to learn the bird's wily ways. In fact, he became one of the few pointing dogs I've owned who mastered this mischievous game bird. He learned to hunt every species of game bird a little differently, and that is much of what makes a dog great.

Still, I have to admit that his very first hunting trip for pheasants wasn't much of a success. Here's what I see in my mind when I think back to that day along an abandoned railroad track near a small town in rural Montana.

The sky was light blue that October morning, with the temperature hovering in the high fifties. A flock of domestic pigeons (rock doves) circled overhead as I parked in the long shadow of a wooden grain elevator. Wheat was scattered on the loading ramp of the "prairie skyscraper," and when I turned off the engine, the pigeons returned to gather the golden grain. Two semi trailers sat on a graveled siding next to the old spur line of the railway.

Sitting in the pickup, my hunting partner Fred pointed a finger toward the rusty steel rails. He was counting the number of ring-necked pheasants sitting on the tracks. The never-ending rails cut through the harvested wheatfields on their way to the parched brown foothills and purple mountains in the distance. Both sides of the railroad bed were thick with brush and high grass. Several small trestles spanned a shallow creek that snaked its way back and forth under the tracks. The lively stream drained the high grassy draws that skirted the edges of the wheatfields. Cattails and willows clogged the low seeps along the waterway.

We sat in the cab eating breakfast. Winston was impatient, so I let him out. The minute he hit the ground he was birdy. Pheasant tracks surrounded the hunting rig, looking as fresh as Winston's paw prints in the moist sand.

"Must be a zillion birds feeding around the elevator," Fred said.

As soon as we stepped onto the tracks, the pheasants along the rail bed vanished. Fred and I walked the same side. He stayed close to the tracks, and I worked a fence-line bordering one of the wheatfields. Winston worked the heavy cover ahead of us. The wet dirt revealed a line of pheasant footprints along the barbed-wire fence, and I saw tall grass waving ahead. Then the cattails moved, but there was no wind.

I walked slowly. Pheasants usually hold fairly tight on opening day of the hunting season, so there was no need to rush. Far in front, a bird flushed now and then for no reason, so I quickened my pace.

Winston slowed down and snapped into a point at the edge of a patch of cattails. Then he continued on. I told myself not to rush, that the birds would flush at the end of the small cattail patch.

I had no idea how many pheasants were in the cattails, but after seeing all the tracks, my knuckles were white from gripping the 20-gauge so tightly. I glanced over at Fred, and he looked like I felt—wide-eyed and shaky. We walked past Winston. He altered position, moving in front of Fred and locking up again. Motionless, we stood on each side of Winston.

Pointing dogs usually "slam to a point" with most game birds, but with pheasants many pointers have a tendency to creep or reposition themselves often. Young Winston was being cautious, but with all the scent around he couldn't stand it any long and dove into the cattails.

There was a thunder of wings, and Fred tumbled the first rooster. Then two more pheasants went out his side, flying across the tracks as he was reloading his double after the first shot. Fred yelled something about being stupid enough to open his gun while birds were in the air. Winston was running around in the cattails like a madman.

Several seconds passed, but it seemed like forever. Then two roosters flushed simultaneously. We both shot, and the birds crashed down beyond the cattails. One bird hit the ground running, with Winston in hot pursuit. Then waves of birds got up and flew down the railroad tracks. We held off shooting, though, to concentrate on the downed bird.

Fred stopped to pick up his first bird, then went after the other dead rooster at the edge of the cattails. Meanwhile, Winston was crashing through a tangle of rose bushes, chasing the winged pheasant. The ringneck ran up the embankment and hoofed it along the tracks,

Winston with a rooster he re-located several times and finally pinned.

with Winston close behind. He dipped his head and scooped up the bird, then came back to me with pride evident in his gait.

"Good dog, good dog," I said as he dropped the big rooster at my feet.

After recovering from the chaos of the last few minutes, Fred and I pushed farther down the tracks after the drove of pheasants. Winston was far out in front now, moving at full speed and flushing a string of pheasants as far as the eye could see.

I turned to Fred with a wry smile, "Sometimes a young dog just has to have a little fun."

Grand Slam

I was on my way to hunt some of North America's most amazing gamebird habitat—a place where a hunter can collect three different species of quail: Mearns', Gambel's, and scaled. If you're fortunate enough to shoot this trio of Southwestern quail, you will have completed a "grand slam." And if you're able to shoot all three species in a single day, I call it a "grand-grand slam," which is something quite difficult to achieve. But that's exactly what I wanted Winston to do that day.

On the approach to Tucson, I looked out the window of the airplane to see a mackerel sky hanging over the Arizona landscape. It took only minutes for the airline attendant to unload my two dogs. After Jeff and I exchanged greetings, we put the dogs and gear in the suburban.

"How are those two pups by Winston doing?" I asked Jeff.

"Great. They're growing like weeds. They're still young, but I hope to start shooting over them before the hunting season ends," Jeff replied.

"I wouldn't share this with many folks, because I'm not someone who brags about dogs, but I must say that Winston is different." I told him. "I've had a lot of dogs, but none that developed so rapidly. I'm not taking anything away from my other dogs, but Winston is extremely intelligent for his age, and he just seems to know how to do things right. It's in his breeding, of course. And maybe the countless hours I've spent with him have accelerated his learning curve.

"Winston makes direct eye contact with me more often than any dog I've ever owned. For most dogs, a fixed stare constitutes a threat, but not for Winston. I believe it's his way of communicating, looking straight in the eyes and really deciphering what I'm saying. This may sound silly, and words really can't describe it, but in my heart we understand each other.

"He does everything I ask him to," I continued. "And in return I try to do the same. Oh, sure, he makes mistakes in the field. But so do I.

"I sure hope one of your pups turns out like Winston."

"Yeah, me to," answered Jeff. "Knowing your dogs, and with Winston being the father, I'm sure there's a good chance it'll happen. But I still don't have your experience with dogs."

"You don't have to. It's in your pups' genes. Just take them hunting, and they'll do the rest."

My Brittany Shoe and I had hunted this ranch before, but for Winston it was going to be a new experience. Jeff had never owned pointing dogs and was new to the ranch, but he wanted to see and hear firsthand how I work pointing dogs in desert country.

I explained to him, "Many hunters hesitate to use dogs in such tough habitat because of the abundance of cacti. But I don't. This hot, dry cactus country and the critters that live here are thought to be hostile to hunting dogs, but there are hazards for dogs everywhere you can hunt birds.

"A person has to have confidence in his dog, as most pointers adapt quite well to desert quail. The biggest disadvantage when hunting desert country is poor scenting conditions much of the year. The dry, sandy soil, heat, and the lack of humidity in arid country all contribute to poor scenting conditions. Make sure your dogs get plenty of water and get it often. Water stimulates a sensitive nose, helping the dog to pick up scent.

"The time of year and day are also factors in helping a dog find birds," I continued. "On some days, nothing seems to work, but if the forecast calls for hot, dry weather and little air movement, I find the most productive time for good scenting conditions to be early morning and late afternoon.

"Also, young game birds don't lay down as much scent as older birds. I'm not sure why, but I know it's true. Maybe it's a young bird's defense mechanism or maybe it's the kind of food consumed while they're developing. We're lucky, because at this time of year the weather is usually cooler and the birds are more mature, making scenting condition better.

"As a rule, when I find a large flock of desert quail, I

scatter them. After the birds are broken up you're in for some great shooting. There is nothing finer than working a pointing dog on a broken covey. This is when a good dog earns its biscuits. In fact, some birds hold so tight for a pointer they may flush unexpectedly, flying up your shirtsleeves. These birds are a pleasure to hunt with a pointing dog."

The weather was changing rapidly as Jeff pulled off the main road. The temperature was in the low sixties and dropping. A west wind followed the meandering roadbed, turning the suburban's tire tracks into snake-like ripples in the loose sand.

The country around us had a lonely, enchanting beauty. It may seem harsh to the untrained observer, but every turn in the road offered a new, breathtaking vista. The golden light had begun to soften the harshness of the sun, transforming the desert into a world of wonder. There was a surprising variety of flora and fauna here, but the two dogs and I would rather see quail than anything else on this trip.

After crossing a sycamore-lined dry creek more times than I could count, we arrived at our destination, an attractive old adobe dwelling. Jeff had done his homework and scouted a few places for birds, but I'd hunted this ranch before and also had my own favorite places for each species of quail.

Jeff was up early the next morning, bringing me a cup of coffee while I fed the dogs. The low morning light was magical, casting long shadows across the cactus-covered landscape.

"Let's start at the Clancy," I told him. "Last year it was full of Gambel's."

"I already checked it out and saw birds. It should be a good place to start."

By the time we arrived at our destination the magic was gone; the wind had picked up and changed direction. The two Brittanys we put down pushed into the wind with heads high and nostrils wide, disappearing quickly into the tall rabbitbrush before Jeff and I even uncased our shotguns.

We followed the direction the dogs took into the rabbitbrush, which was a soft amber color now that the pale green foliage was gone. A sandy two-rut track led us toward a whirling windmill. Winston and Shoe had already visited the water tank when Jeff and I arrived, and their bellies dripped water as they crisscrossed the sandy trail in front of us. Beyond the tank, we followed the sounds of the beepers in the high rabbitbrush. A single Gambel's quail flushed wild at my feet. Startled, I didn't mount the gun, but followed the bird with my eyes and marked it down on a grassy slope high above me.

Quail tracks were everywhere in the sand. Then I spotted the birds dashing ahead on the ground, the dogs in hot pursuit. Both Brittanys pointed, then moved, then stopped and moved again; their beepers changing from the pointing mode to the running mode each time they shifted positions.

Finally, they caught up to the large bunch of Gambel's milling around in heavy cover, and there was a tremendous roar of wings. Some of the birds followed the wash, others went in the direction the early-flushing single took.

I marked several birds down and saw others running up the hill. Winston also knew the birds' approximate location, and by the time Jeff and I got there, he was locked up on point. As Jeff walked in front of Winston, a single quail peeled off down the hill in the direction of the wash. Winston followed the single, and Jeff held up until the bird cleared the dog and then fired. Winston retrieved the quail to me and I handed it to Jeff.

"Nice shot, Jeff," I said and shook his hand.

He looked over the beautiful male Gambel's quail several times, then slipped it into his vest.

Shoe came running from the bottom of the arroyo.

"Shoe must have been pointing in the heavy rabbit-brush. I'm surprised he broke point after the shot. Normally, he wouldn't have. But maybe the bird he was on flushed when you shot."

"I never heard his beeper sound. Did you, Ben?"

"No, but the wind funneling down the wash probably covered the sound."

Shoe came toward us, then stopped dead in his tracks, his eyes fixed ten steps ahead.

"The quail is between you and the dog, Jeff. Walk straight to Shoe. I'm going to check on Winston. The last time I heard his beeper was on the ridge above us."

Walking up the slope, I heard the beeper in pointing mode, then saw Winston pointing in front of some mesquite brush. I heard Jeff shoot down below just as three Gambel's ran out the other side of the mesquite and flushed. I tagged one bird, adding the echo of my shot to Jeff's.

Between us, we collected six birds from the large covey. And the two dogs had an equal share of the work.

"Ben, let's try to get a Mearns' quail for Winston. There is a place not far from here—maybe twenty minutes—where a cowboy said he saw a covey of Mearns' by a water tank."

"Is it Passage Tank?"

"No, it's Mesquite Tank, two miles above Passage Tank, toward the palisades."

"That looks like good quail county, but I've never walked that high. I'm all for it. Let's go."

We drove through a river of sand, following a dry two-track toward the high mountains. The lane twisted and turned along the riparian wash. The dry sandy arroyos owed like rivers from the mountain palisades to the valley floor. The mesquite savanna shaped the foothills, and a backdrop of dark evergreen oaks softened the landscape as it climbed into the sky.

Having hunted Mearns' quail before, I knew their routine begins not long after sunrise. The birds generally forage uphill and continue feeding throughout the day. They pause and rest during midday. After filling their crops in the evening, they slowly descend, almost touching one another.

There was not a cloud in the sky when we arrived, not a breath of wind. Long shadows covered much of the wide grassy arroyo. Jeff shut off the engine and we sat in silence, transfixed by the view of the rocky palisades. The low light had transformed them into a medieval rampart.

I glanced at Jeff, then back to the fortress. "Do you think it's possible to get a Mearns' quail here and then go for a scaled quail too?" I asked him.

"I'm not sure. We have maybe two hours left to hunt."

"I don't like breaking up a covey after five o'clock. They need time to get back together to feed before sunset. So that gives us even less time. At this time of day the Mearns' should be working their way downhill, so let's concentrate on the grassy sidehills of the arroyo. And look for diggings, as Mearns' quail feed exclusively on the ground and use their stout legs and long claws to scratch."

"What are diggings?" asked Jeff.

"This time of year, Mearns' quail feed mostly on bulbs and tubers from plants they dig up, such as chufa, sometimes called nutgrass and carex, which is a sedge. In years of good mast crops, they feed on acorns from evergreen oaks. The diggings are distinctive and deep, about the size of your fist. When foraging, the birds feed together so look for lots of holes.

"Let's get going, and if I find some diggings, I'll show you. Today, we won't go that high into the mountains. We'll start right here and hunt the shrub-grassland. Most folks who hunt Mearns' quail think you have to go to the oaks in the mountains for good hunting, but lower grasslands that have not been overgrazed also hold birds. But it's essential to have a good grassy understory for food and cover."

A tired Winston with singles from broken coveys.

We released the dogs and within seconds both Brittanys locked up solid on a huge covey of running Gambel's quail. The birds dodged in and out of the tall rabbitbrush. Shoe and Winston worked ahead of us, and each time we moved past them, they repositioned and pointed again. Finally, the covey flushed, flying up the steep grade and out of sight. Neither of us shot. I'd hunt them another day.

As we continued to walk along, I said to Jeff, "In my experience, Mearns' quail lie great for pointing dogs. If they're in the right cover, a covey may react to danger by freezing when approached. But they'll also spread out and hoof it at times. They're strong runners, but when pursued, birds usually run only a short distance before hiding or flushing. Once flushed, singles will also run after landing, looking for a good tuft of grass to hide in."

The dogs slammed into a point in front of us. Jeff quickened his pace, his shotgun held tightly and his eyes darting from Winston to Shoe. In a low voice, I called to him to slow down, but he didn't seem to hear. He moved past the frozen dogs, but no birds flushed.

"Jeff, turn around," I said.

He stepped back and a single flushed under his feet. "Gambel's," I cried out as he dumped the quail at twenty feet. He's a good shot, but he kept reminding me he's not. No one really has to tell you if they're good or poor, though, as the proof rests in the game pockets of their vests.

Jeff walked over and handed me the male quail after wrestling the bird away from Winston, who of course thinks every bird belongs to me.

"I thought it was a…" He stopped short of finishing the sentence, still looking at the beautiful Gambel's quail.

"I was thinking Mearns' myself, because the dogs held so tight even after we walked by."

Jeff slipped the quail into his vest pouch.

The winter sun was low in the sky, but still warm. We walked on to Mesquite Creek Tank. The dogs piled in, splashing muddy water in the air.

"Quail tracks, but no diggings," I softly announced to Jeff. "You can't always tell, but Gambel's quail leave lots of tracks and fan out when traveling. Mearns' coveys have fewer tracks with larger footprints, and they travel closer together."

My eyes followed the direction of the quail tracks, and a hundred yards ahead I spotted the wet, dripping dogs standing motionless. "More Gambel's running ahead," I announced.

I called the dogs and they came reluctantly. We back-tracked so the dogs could get another drink before we changed direction.

After a twenty-minute walk, the evergreen oak foothills seemed no closer. But I did find the first diggings and called Jeff over to see them.

"The ground looks like it's been excavated by turkeys or javelina, but I'm sure it's Mearns' quail, as the holes are small and close together," I explained.

A short distance farther on we found more scratching and diggings. "The quail are close by, so it's just a matter of time now."

Winston and Shoe found them while running in tandem down a steep, rocky ravine. Both Brittanys twisted 180 degrees as they locked up, their heads almost touching their tails. Eight or ten Mearns' quail flushed wild, scattering in two directions. Jeff and I were awestruck by the wild flush and did nothing but watch the birds disappear over a hill.

The dogs remained on point, so I whispered, "Walk, don't run, it should be a single. Walk past Winston. The bird is all yours, Jeff."

Two Mearns' quail bust out of the cover then tumbled to the ground in unison with the sound of the shots. The dogs retrieved the birds to me. Both were fine-looking Mearns' roosters.

The sun was sinking behind the mountains when we reached the suburban. On days like this, you just wish for another hour of daylight.

Jeff and I pulled the quail from our vests and softly smoothed their feathers, admiring the beautiful birds. We lay the Gambel's and Mearns' quail down in a row, and their bodies cast long shadows on the sand. The wind swept from the palisades toward the valley below, toward home. And I made a promise to Winston that we'd finish our grand slam during tomorrow's hunt.

In Savannah Country

Many folks think of the Southwestern desert as little more than a wasteland, so it may come as a surprise to discover that savannahs also exist here. Desert savannas are ecosystems with continuous grass and scattered trees or shrubs. This is scaled quail country, and the birds move like a soft desert breeze—one day they're all around you; the next they're gone.

That day, Jeff and I were after scaled quail, and we had moved farther away from Gambel's and Mearns' habitat. Jeff turned off the main gravel road onto a dirt lane that wandered through a series of grassy draws then upward to an open savannah. We left the suburban parked in the shadow of an old windmill that feeds water to a tank. Water is the lifeline of the savannah, and almost every living creature visits tanks like this one periodically.

As we went through the routine of getting our gear in order—guns, dogs, beeper collars—Jeff asked, "When was the first time you hunted scaled quail?"

"Further back than I care to remember," was my first response. "Time, every now and then, scares the heck out of me. The radio was playing Peter, Paul, and Mary on my first western quail hunt. But it was later, in Oklahoma, when I saw my first bunch of scaled quail along an old grass-covered dirt road.

"I had been hunting bobwhites in eastern Oklahoma and was heading back home through the western part of the state when I stopped to find some scaled quail. After a successful hunt, I stopped at a small-town cafe and heard a different story about scaled quail.

"A deer hunter—I could tell by his outfit—sat down at the counter on the next stool, looked me up and down, and said, 'Is that your huntin' rig with the two dogs?' I nodded my head. 'You can't hunt scalies with bird dogs. They're runners and dogs can't keep up with them.' I nodded again agreeably, and he finished his coffee, wished me well, and walked out the door with a big grin on his face. A year later, I returned to western Oklahoma and had superb scaled quail hunting with my dogs. His opinion mirrored that of most hunters at the time—and even today."

The windmill towered over the grasslands like a rusty skyscraper; a long steel pipe spewed crystal-clear water into a long concrete stock tank. The dogs jumped in belly deep to take advantage of the cool water.

The sound of the windmill's turning blades and grinding gears was carried down to us on the breeze. It rippled along an old adobe wall, part of a dwelling made long ago by the first residents to use the clear water. As I put the beeper collars on the dogs, I wondered how long those first settlers lasted out here.

The sweet smell of fragrant desert plants surrounded us. Winston and Shoe scented the air and disappeared into the main draw. We walked four hundred yards before turning uphill to cross the ridge and then started down the other side. We were walking the sidehill when we saw Shoe planted like a white stone in the grass. Then he moved slowly forward, step by step. He stopped again, and this time never moved a muscle. Head held high, he inhaled the scent.

I sensed the birds' presence, but I had no idea if they were Gambel's or scalies, even though the habitat read scaled quail.

Winston crested the ridge and moved downslope with the wind. He saw Shoe and slammed on the brakes—a bit late. The grass exploded under his feet as a huge covey of scaled quail burst skyward and flew across the draw, setting down on an open grassy bench several hundred yards away. Winston seemed surprised and looked at me for forgiveness. I waved him on, knowing he did nothing wrong. Then he ran full speed in the direction of the quail, and I whistled him back.

A moist breeze kicked up and scenting conditions changed for the better. The birds seemed glued to the ground, and both dogs made a number of great points as we broke up the birds. Together we killed half a dozen scaled quail, enough for any hunt.

We returned to the windmill to gut the birds and clean them in the clear cool water. Over lunch, we both agreed that hunting scaled quail is rarely this easy.

Jeff and I shared one more day in the field before he

had to get back to work. But we made a plan to get back together later in the week. In the meantime, I had arranged to hunt with another friend of mine.

I had met Jim Bob on the ranch the previous year, and we had discussed hunting together, but that never materialized. So this year I made it a point to take him hunting. Jim Bob is a cowboy in every sense of the word. His adobe is near the Mexican border, and once sheltered a variety of banditos. It was a robber's roost, and the story goes that even Pancho Villa stayed there several times.

I pulled up in the shadow of the sycamores near Jim Bob's adobe and waited for him to return. Lunch had come and gone by the time he slid the bridle off the head of his big mare. She blinked and slowly walked away, a patch of sweat marking where the saddle blanket had lain on her back. Their trip had started before dawn, and both she and the rider were glad to be back at the ranch. But there was no hurry. Hunting Rustler's Well is best late in the day, anyway.

Since childhood, Jim Bob's expertise has been honed from the back of a horse. Between rounding up yearling calves and trailing mountain lions with his pack of redbone hounds, he knows every canyon and has traversed every mountain in the area, keeping a detailed map in his head. Jim Bob is a horseman first and a dogman second, but with great respect for all working animals. But this day he doesn't know what to expect, as he's never hunted quail, never seen pointing dogs work, and doesn't even own a shotgun.

As we drove toward our hunting destination, I said, "The cover looks good, Jim Bob. What kind of gray-green grass is that?"

"Tobosa grass."

"Is it good for livestock?"

"The cattle wouldn't eat it even if you put molasses syrup on it."

I laughed, thinking to myself that it looked like good quail cover.

Jim Bob interrupted my thoughts by pointing a finger out the window. "Look, there's a few wild pigs. Years ago I caught a mean feral piglet to raise for meat. He was even mean when I fed him. And you know what, Ben, when I put him in the freezer he was still mean."

Jim Bob laughed then spit out the window.

I was still chuckling when we stopped next to Rustler's Well. Each year I look forward to hunting here. The windmill's fins use even the slightest breeze to lift the liquid gold up from the depths to the dry desert above. A large eight-foot steel tank holds tons of pure, precious water, and an overflow pipe fills the small reservoir. Lush green plants skirt the pond, ones that can't adapt to the hot, dry desert. It's an oasis for surrounding creatures, large and small.

We sat in the pickup for a minute, watching a covey of Gambel's and a covey of scalies run for cover. Both coveys used the same escape route, zigzagging from one mesquite bush to another. My eyes never left the moving birds, and when I could no longer see them, I glanced over at Jim Bob.

He looked at me in amazement for a moment then spoke: "That's a lot of birds! What's your plan?"

"When I lost sight of the birds on the ground, they were dividing into small groups," I started. "I don't know if you noticed, but the scaled quail didn't go toward the arroyo, but moved more to the right, staying in the mesquite grasslands. The Gambel's quail fanned out but kept going toward the wash. Let's finish our coffee and I'll explain my plan.

"Pointing dogs work great on desert quail, but the most important thing is to walk slowly and let the dogs work the group after they fan out."

The first shot came within minutes of leaving the hunting rig. The dogs stacked up like a couple of dominos about to fall. Jim Bob laughed when he missed his first shot, and then laughed again when two more birds flushed just as he opened the side-by-side to reload.

Before Winston and Shoe got to the sandy wash, I called them in. We circled back, finding a dozen more scaled quail out in the grassy savannah. Jim Bob laughed every time he shot. He was having the time of his life, but putting no birds in his vest.

On two more passes through the same area we found more scattered singles and Jim Bob's shooting improved.

Later, Winston worked a bunch of Gambel's quail that were running toward the wash. A light wind picked up, and it wasn't long before Winston slowed, then stopped facing a large patch of high rabbitbrush. I signaled to Jim Bob where I thought the birds were, but they flushed out of gun range. The quail banked and

Winston and his kennelmates scan the desert savannah.
Winston with a scaled quail (below).

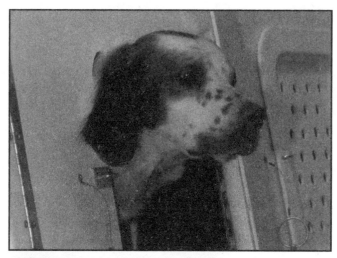

Eager (above), and fulfilled and tired (left).

came screaming past us, and both of us killed an incoming bird. Still laughing, Jim Bob took a long second shot and missed. He was happy with the first shot and smiled when Winston brought the bird back to me. Most of the birds had own low over the rabbitbrush, fanning out and then landing.

We worked slowly downwind for the next two hundred yards, encouraging the dogs to work the high cover. The singles were almost impossible to find, but we managed to kill two more birds.

Farther down the dry wash, the wind got stronger, kicking up small particles of sand and bending the dry golden grass to its roots. The dogs found a couple of scaled quail as we looped back along a hillside, but we didn't get a shot.

On the walk back, I congratulated Jim Bob on killing his first scaled and Gambel's quail. "Not bad for your first time bird hunting. You're the first person I've ever taken to Rustler's Well, which is a special place for me.

"Years ago an old cowboy drew the whereabouts of the well in the sand for me. Minutes later a dust devil erased its location, almost before I could commit it to memory. I thought to myself, 'Maybe it still has something to hide.'

"I've found that there are usually scaled and Gambel's quail around the reservoir. Each time I stop, the birds scurry toward that low arroyo wash. The dogs and I used to take off after them in hot pursuit. We'd find a few birds, but most seemed to vanish into the heart of the desert.

"We'd work the birds as fast as possible. Point, hurry, run; point, hurry, run. This worked, but the end result was always the same. The dogs would scent only one or two birds.

"Several years ago I watched a large covey of quail running ahead of me. I was on a high landform, looking down at them. The birds divided into smaller and smaller groups and then gathered back together where they first separated. It finally occurred to me that desert quail fan out as they run—just as they do when flushed—and then get back together as soon as possible. They're biologically programmed to do this for their very survival.

"And, Jim Bob, that's why I now hunt them the way I do."

Laughing, Jim Bob replied, "Well, Ben, it seems to work."

Back at the hunting rig, I asked Jim Bob if he'd like a beer.

He answered yes, so I asked, "What kind of beer do you like?"

"Two kinds," he said, laughing. "Cold beer and free beer."

Driving the suburban back to where I was staying, I thought that Winston finally did get his grand slam. But not a grand-grand slam—that would come later.

Epilogue

Winston started toward greatness in a hurry. And looking back now, there may have been a reason. Most Brittanys live to the ripe old age of fourteen or fifteen years. But Winston died at just eight years, seven months, and a few days. After his death, I scattered his ashes over the landscape in the places I thought he liked best. It took a long time before I felt comfortable walking the same ground again.

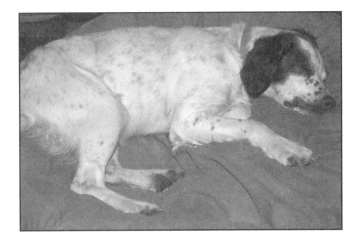